THE 5 ½ MILE HIGH CLUB

The
5 1⁄2

MILE HIGH CLUB

Uncovering a Missing Step
in Modern Christianity

Craig P. Wendel

Printed in the United States of America

First Printing, 2016

ISBN 978-0692653586

Book and Cover design by Vina Howell

Photography by Jacqui Ray Tello

Note: Names and details in the stories in this book have been changed to protect anonymity.

DEDICATION

To my Dad, the man who raised me in an amazing home and
showed me how to be a solid man of God.

PRAISE FOR THE 5 ½ MILE HIGH CLUB

Craig Wendel is a lover of God and a lover of people and is one of the sharpest thinkers on how to bring the two together. For years I have admired his calm, yet passionate leadership style. When you walk through the door of his church on a Sunday morning you are confronted with one rich story after another. Stories of people who have been led well on a spiritual journey up a great mountain and experienced the view. Read this book, and you may find yourself on a similar journey to new places and heights in your relationship with the Lord. Craig, thanks for your investment in pastors and leaders of this generation. You are one of the great Sherpas you've aspired to be.

-Michael W Smith
ARC
Director of Church Planting
www.arcchurches.com

In reading this creative, witty and impactful book, you will quickly become aware of the "what, how, and why" of the upward journey of life. It has been my privilege to climb part of this life with Craig Wendel. He has been to the mountain top and is now leading many others to experience the same. So "Let us go up to the mountain of the Lord."

-Andrew DeLong
Pastor of Tree of Life Church
Naples, FL

Do you have a relationship that you are so grateful for, but feel like you don't appreciate it as much as you should? That relationship is my friendship with Craig Wendel. I have known him for over 10 years and don't know anyone who is more committed to leading people to experience all that God has for them like he is.

You can tell by the way he relates to people, either one on one or on the stage, he wants more for God's people! This book is like reading Craig's heart for you and for me. This book is smart, witty and an authentic challenge to christians everywhere to humbly and passionately pursue all that God has for them.

-Naeem Fazal
Author of Ex-Muslim
Pastor of Mosaic Church

Craig Wendel's love for people is genuine and whenever he is in the presence of others, church happens - it just happens so naturally. With this book, Craig unpacks the wisdom of the Sherpa with personal stories that made me laugh really hard and caused me to pause and reflect on the depth of his experiences. He has bravely climbed a few steps ahead and is leading, so intentionally, the pastors and leaders journeying on the path he's forged.

-Pierre du Plessis
Pastor of Father's House Church

"I'm excited to recommend this extraordinary book where my good friend connects the dots to living beyond yourself! The legacy you leave must empower others to do what they're called to do. In The 5 1/2 Mile High Club, Craig gives us action steps to help others find the joy of making it to the top in their relationship with Christ."

-Hal Hardy
Pastor of Highlands Church

CONTENTS

ACKNOWLEDGMENTS

Special thanks to Ashley for making me sound smarter than I am.

INTRODUCTION

When I walked into the borrowed condominium, it smelled like old people and the furniture was straight out of a *Leave It to Beaver* episode, decorated from the catalogues of *Home Interiors* circa 1970. Even though it wasn't up to my hipster design feel, the place had a view that was spectacular. One entire wall was nothing but glass that showed off the most gorgeous thing around: the view. Our little vacation getaway was perched on the edge of the sand that ran out to the lazy waves of the Gulf of Mexico. Just a couple of steps beyond the glass wall and your little tootsies were buried deep in the sugary sand of South Florida.

I hate sand. I hate the beach. Sand is like syrup; once it's opened it's everywhere. One step onto the beach and even your unborn children are covered in sand, it's a fact! So, even though I loved the free place to stay, and I was enamored with the view, I wasn't going outside. As I sat in a hard, plastic covered, Naugahyde recliner, I scanned the shelves looking for something to read to pass the time. There, sandwiched in between two classic books, was a shiny paperback book that looked promising. It was John Krakauer's book, *Into Thin Air*.

Up until that point I had never heard of Sherpas or even knew that they existed. I was totally clueless as to their superhuman feats on the mountain at that extemporaneous elevation. To be honest, the book was not focused on the Sherpas, but is instead an epic true-life tale of a mountain climbing disaster that happened on Mt. Everest in the mid nineties. Although Krakauer's story was fascinating, my mind stayed locked into the Sherpa guides and the things that they did for the climbers that were under their care. Climbers used and benefited from things on the mountain that seem to have mysteriously appeared. Safety ropes that went all the way to the top, oxygen tanks spaced evenly up the trail, and even tents that were setup before the climbers arrived. I read between every line of the book, seeing how this mysteriously new breed of superhuman people were accomplishing amazing feats of heroism everyday, just so the climbers in the lime light could summit Mt. Everest. Of course, the climbers that made it to the top celebrated and had their photos snapped at the top of the world, and I knew who was holding the camera. It was the same Sherpa that ran the safety rope, transported the oxygen tanks and carried more than their entire body weight in gear and equipment. These Sherpas easily held the camera and took photos of the neophytes on the summit, because they had already been there several times prior to that moment to prepare the way for those that had not yet arrived.

I knew at that moment that I wanted to be a Sherpa. I wanted to do whatever it took to help, coach, coax, cajole, and even carry as many people to the top of their spiritual life as possible. The adventure for me was not to spiritually summit again and again, but to help someone else experience it, and watch their face as their eyes lit up with the thrill of standing on the pinnacle of their spiritual existence. To finally understand what it meant and felt like to have a spiritual encounter with Jesus Christ and to come away changed.

I read the entire book in what seemed like a breath, and as I turned the final page and closed the book, an entirely new area of my life opened up. For some strange reason that novel about mountain climbing and a report on an excruciatingly tragic event at 10,000 feet helped unwrap a mystery in my spiritual journey. At that point in my life I had been following Jesus for nearly two decades. As a full time minister for one of those decades it had become a job instead of a passionate pursuit of serving the One that changed my life. Time had eroded away at the razor edge of commitment that I used to have, leaving me with only a dull sense of what was really happening around me. As I attempted to excel and climb the proverbial ladder of success that exists in church world, I found myself becoming less and less engaged in the passionate thing that at one time took my breath away. It wasn't until I started researching and studying the amazing Sherpa people that layers of my own selfish inadequacies began to unfold revealing the heart of a man that had almost completely fallen prey to the misdirection of the enemy that wants to lead everyone to the same conclusion: that it's all about *us*. When in fact, Jesus said it's all about *them*.

1
THE PATH

I'M A GUY, AND BECAUSE of that, I realize that I am not the sharpest tool in the shed. In fact, more times than not, I allow adrenaline and the hope of adventure propel me into areas and situations that I really should have been smart enough to avoid, but time and time again, like most guys, I find myself standing in the middle of a train wreck laughing at myself. Like the time my buddy and I decided to pull my 1982 loser blue Chevette over in a ditch to jump on a moving cargo train that was lumbering by. At the time it sounded like an amazing adventure, never mind the risk of falling and losing both legs under the steel wheels of the train...how would I explain that to my parents? The non-forward-thinking guy in me never processed the idea that once you jump on the train how do you get off? Where do you get off? How far away will your chick magnet car be when the train comes to its final destination in Detroit, Michigan which is two hours away from where you jumped on? Yep, I'm a guy. Long term processing fails to overcome the immediate surge of the toxic concoction of testosterone and adrenaline. So finding myself mostly naked, hanging on a cliff face, in a rainforest jungle in Central America is totally plausible.

It wasn't my plan to be half naked hanging from a cliff in the rain forest. My plan was to take my team of teenagers swimming in a river in the Jungle for a fun and relaxing afternoon. We had already been in Honduras for five days working long hours in the hot, steamy sun of a remote village named Rio Viejo working on a church building. This was our one day of relaxation before hopping on a plane and heading back to the States.

I hate sand and I dislike water. It's just not my cup of tea. But, after numerous days of being sticky, sweaty, and funky, I was actually looking forward to swimming. Our swimming area was something out of the movie Blue Lagoon, minus the naked teenagers and pitiful dialogue of course. It was a wide river flowing in-between two cliff walls that rose about a hundred feet or so on each side; it was picturesque. I swam for a bit and then dragged my scrawny, tired body up on a wide, flat rock that was in the middle of the river. The rock had been warmed by the sun and was an awesome contrast to the chilly mountain river water that flowed around it. I had sat there for about five minutes when he swam over and unceremoniously hauled himself up on the rock next to me with a sloppy splash.

You know that guy that's annoying? That guy that you do your best to avoid? You can't really put your finger on what makes him so annoying, but all you know is that you would rather have your pants filled with rabid squirrels than have to spend time with that guy. Well, that guy happened to be Adam, and Adam was our American intern that was living in Honduras at the time, and was hosting our small band of wannabe missionaries.

The minute he landed on my Plymouth Rock he started, "Hey you wanna climb that cliff? I can show you how. I've climbed it a dozen times, it's easy, and even you can do it."

It was that last, "even you could do it" that caused dangerous levels of testosterone and adrenaline to surge through my veins, causing my long term processors and common sense to short circuit.

"Of course I can scale that cliff!" The words coming out of my mouth tasted like a deep fried stick of butter. Rich and flavorful at first, but then followed by panic and fear as I felt my heart stopping under the weight of the internal sludge. I couldn't believe I had just said that!

Adam's response was quick and poignant. He slipped in the water and said, "Follow me. I'll show you how to do it."

Obviously, I had no choice in the matter, since now my man card had been put on the auction block of life.

We got to the bottom of the cliff and stepped up on a small, slippery ledge that was just below the water line. Adam looked at me and said, "Okay all you have to do is do what I do. I'll show you where to put each of your hands and where to place your feet, and then we will be at the top in no time." I put my hand out and touched the warm hard rock that was looming to the heavens, and I craned my neck back to see exactly how high it was. You know how they always say don't look down when you are up really high because it will make you either fall or wet yourself? From experience, let me just tell you that being at the bottom of a cliff and looking up has the same effect.

Standing there in nothing but a swimsuit and fresh urine, I chose crazy over common sense and started to climb. The first twenty feet or so were relatively easy. Adam would advance a few feet, then pause and look back at me, telling me where to hold, when to lean, how to lean, and different places to put my feet. I never could have made it if it weren't for his confident coaching. In those first twenty feet, the annoying guy from the rock had morphed into a guy that I was depending on for each and every step. I was advancing, but it was also a bit painful here and there. The rocks were starting to cut into my soft, bare feet, and my hands were starting to cramp, but Adam continued to encourage me and point out different ways and places to hold and hang to heft my scrawny body up higher and higher. With each foot and handhold I was feeling more and more like a pro, until about fifty feet up in the air. Adam looked back at me and said, "Okay this is the tricky part, you have to trust me."

Trust him? What did he think I had been doing? It wasn't like I had been ignoring him or mocking him up until this point! The only reason I was mostly naked, hanging on a cliff face, in a rainforest jungle in Central America was because I trusted him.

Adam and I were side by side on a small crack. The crack was just deep enough to have our toes jammed in it to support our weight. He shifted his body weight, leaning close to me, and then like a sling shot he lunged himself in the opposite direction letting go of the rock face completely and hurtling his body over a void in the cliff, to re-attach himself about four feet away on the other side of the void. He looked back at me and said, "Just do exactly what I did, you got this man."

I thought I had emptied all of my bladder at the bottom of the cliff, but hanging there, half naked on a cliff wall in the rainforest, I found more fluids that were obviously no longer needed inside my body. The very thought of letting go of this gorgeous, solid rock to fly through the air a million feet above a raging river not only *sounded* ridiculous, I *knew* it was.

I inched forward and was standing at the place where Adam had launched himself across the void and into a whole new level of admiration in my mind. Adam was now only about four feet away from me, but those four feet might as well have been a mile. Too far to reach; too close to need a jetpack. Adam said, "Come on man you can do this. It's not near as hard as it looks. You just have to push hard and commit yourself to go the distance."

The only distance I could think of was the distance down to the water below and my frail, half naked body, careening down the cliff, bouncing off of little outcroppings until it splattered against the water far below. Melodramatic I know, but it was enough to make me quit. The leap of faith was too much, I chickened out. "I can't do it man. I'm going back down." With that simple declaration I began my slow descent back down to the waters edge where all the little people dwelled.

Adam had been to the top of that cliff numerous times. In fact, he had been up and down so many times it wasn't even challenging for him anymore. There was no risk or testing of his skill, but he had discovered where the new thrill was. He found out what he had to do to make the same climb exciting and enjoyable, and that was to take somebody with him.

What he was trying to help me accomplish is the same thing that the Sherpa people do every day of their lives. The Sherpas are an amazing people group that are born at such a high elevation that their bodies are conditioned from birth to do extraordinary things at high altitude. Their amazing skillset and great strength is recognized by anyone who ventures to that part of the world. The first summit of Mt. Everest by Sir Edmund Hillary on May 29, 1953 was accomplished due to the heroic efforts of his Sherpa climbing partner, Tenzing Norgay. That was of course decades ago and now it is unheard of and impossible to summit Mt. Everest or K2 without the help of a Sherpa.

Sherpas have unparalleled abilities at high altitude, often times carrying gear and equipment that is equivalent to their own body weight. They set safety ropes from the base camp all the way up to the summit, affixing ladders over crevasses, and even distributing oxygen bottles up the climb at strategic points for their climbing clients. The Sherpas take responsibility for the health, safety, and safe return of those under their care. They even summit the mountain numerous times to prepare the way so that somebody else can summit successfully once.

Spiritually, to summit, is discovering a relationship with Jesus Christ, which is the single most poignant moment in anybody's life. The feeling that happens when you first open up your mind, heart, and soul to Jesus is hard to explain. I have seen some people laugh while others might cry uncontrollably. One guy that I prayed with to accept Christ just stood there with his mouth hanging open in shock. I asked him if everything was okay, and he stammered, "I just never knew it would be like this. I'm overwhelmed." No matter what emotion

And within that seed of awesomeness, lays an issue that has stymied the church for centuries. bubbles to the top, one thing is for sure, there is nothing like it, and that's awesome. And within that seed of awesomeness, lays an issue that has stymied the church for centuries.

The problem with this whole idea is that with any great feeling, we want to quickly consume that moment and then tackle what's next. We are a 'what's next?' generation. We move effortlessly from one over the top experience to the next, barely slowing down to digest the one we just had. But there is nothing higher nor greater than Christ; He truly is the pinnacle. So any step in any direction is a step backwards. That never stops anybody though, since we seem to have this 'next step' concept hardwired into our DNA from birth.

Growing up in the church, I have seen scores of people start with Christ and then become bored and drift away. Either the seed fell on stony ground, or it was choked out by the cares of life. But one way or the other it didn't grow, and the Christian walk that began as an exciting mountain top experience quickly morphs into a predictable, non-tantalizing, life long journey that is simply miserable. John was one of these *drifters*.

DRIFTERS

When John first came into my youth group (many years ago), he was a pimply faced, greasy haired kid. His clothes were mismatched and he had funky body odor that reminded you of cooking chitlins on a hot summer day, with all the windows closed and no ventilation. He was clueless as to anything about church, Jesus, or hygiene. But over the next few weeks, he formed less awkward relationships with the other teens and not only discovered what soap was, he also discovered Christ. He found himself standing at the top of the spiritual mountain where he made his mark. It was awesome to seem him standing there with his flag of identity planted deep in the cold ice and snow of his melting soul as he boldly declared that he was a follower of Jesus.

Over the next two years, I watched him grow in the church. His circle of influence grew, and in church world, his cool factor grew as well. It wasn't long until John found himself a girlfriend. And it wasn't long after that, John discovered this thing called sex. At least that's what the kids were calling it back then; plain and simple, no code words or catchy phrases, just sex. Nowadays, there are so many different ways to refer to it that you have to be careful using certain common words and phrases. I needed to meet with this one guy, so I said, "Hey man, you wanna hook up this weekend?" and he said, "Dude, I'm not like that."

John reached a life changing moment, where he saw everything so clearly, that he altered his course. He moved from the wide and dismal path he was on, to the crystalline and narrow path of Christ. It changed him and he loved the change in his life, until the insatiable desire to achieve again kicked at his door, until the boredom and monotony of church under-whelmed him. It was then that a simple, basic, new discovery in his life outshined the fading novelty of his last summit appearance.

> He moved from the wide and dismal path he was on, to the crystalline and narrow path of Christ.

REPEATERS

The other thing I have seen in my long tenure in church world is God-fearing people who follow Jesus with all their hearts, attempt to go from one summit experience to the next. They do everything within their power to repeat their last spiritual experience. They drive around, surfing the web, reading books, and indulging themselves in the latest fad or new thing coming out of the Church world. Usually, these exuberant people always start with the passage of Scripture that says, "Behold, I am doing a new thing," and then they are off to seek their next "summit experience," full of gusto, at least until the novelty wears off. Then, they find something else to indulge in, doing their best to make sure each new high is greater than the last.

This was never clearer than when I ministered in a Charismatic church that had all the bells, whistles, and accoutrements that you could imagine. I always said that if you could find it or make it, we would wave it high in the air like we just don't care. In every Sunday service, we would make sure that we had banners, streamers, tambourines, shofars (of course, when blown, filled the sanctuary with a vivid dead animal smell that was akin to a redneck hunting excursion gone wrong), cymbals, finger symbols, knee cymbals (no, I'm not kidding!), headbands, special worship shoes, flag teams, dancers, and who could forget the special intercessor/dancer uniform. These church services looked a whole lot like a cross between Cirque du Soleil and a gypsy wedding.

> If you could find it or make it, we would wave it high in the air like we just don't care.

All of these people were incredibly sincere with an amazing passion for God. They were not heretics or even mentally unstable. They were God fearing, God loving people who found themselves seeking their next summit experience, their next spiritual adventure where they could reach that apex, and then plant their proverbial flag. Sadly, many are still looking in the wrong places.

FLAGGERS

Since I'm a professional church-goer, I know what both a drifter and a repeater look like, because I have experienced both myself, but that's not all. I've also been a flagger. I've flagged for years. In fact, you could go ahead and say that I was raised by flaggers, in an environment that bred flaggers.

I climbed the exact same mountain and planted the exact same flag over and over again. I've been "saved" more times than Elizabeth Taylor's and Larry King's marriages, *combined!* The crazy thing is that this type of stagnated Christianity is still perpetuated even today. You go to church and listen to the minister and you know he is coming to a close not because he said, "now in closing," (because we all know that doesn't mean jack), but because he starts telling you that you might die today. You might walk out of here and get run over by a truck. In all my years growing up in church I have heard the exact same altar call given by hundreds of ministers and not once did I ever hear that I might get run over by a Prius; always a bus, sometimes a truck, but never a Prius. A Prius just doesn't seem to scream pain like a dump truck full of bibles.

Fear is a powerful motivator that will cause you to question your salvation and drive you to the altar, which in turn, makes the minister feel like he has done a good job, because someone decided to give their life to the Lord. One of the problems of using fear to motivate is that it perpetuates a flagger lifestyle. It creates the thought that I should go down front 'one more time' just to make sure all is right with my soul. We mean well, but in reality our flagger mentality actually decreases our confidence in the saving, sustaining grace of God and perpetuates a rule abiding lifestyle where we have to earn our salvation.

We walk the walk to the front because we are motivated by fear that we did something last week that has caused us to lose our salvation, and since we lost our salvation then obviously God is sending a truck our way, not a Prius, a truck. Nobody wants to get hit by a truck. What this instills in us then, is the insidious idea that our salvation is earned and maintained by works instead of by grace. Our faith walk through life then becomes focused on adhering to rules and regulations instead of perpetuating our relationship with Jesus. I know many people that adhere to a list of rules and think they are just fine, but they have no real, passionate relationship with Jesus. The scary thing is that Jesus said that He was going to look at a lot of people on the big day and say, "You followed a lot of rules. You learned the playbook and did a lot of really neat stuff. But I don't know you, and you don't know me."

When I was 8 years old I was in the typical children's church at my home church. It was a great program with a lot of kids and the leaders genuinely loved the kids they were teaching. I felt it and loved it, all except for one terrifying Sunday morning when I became a flagger.

Sister Shirley[1] stood up and said, "Okay boys and girls today we are not going to have a lesson or puppets. Today we are going to have a little drama."

So, out walks this big guy from the church who sat down on a big chair and he was dressed in all white with a cheesy fake Santa beard. Then, he opened a book and started calling out some of our names. Different kids would walk up and he would feign looking for their names in the book that sat in front of him. I was pretty sure it was a dictionary. The first two kids' names were found, so the big albino Santa smiled and said, "Welcome" and then they got to walk through the door on the right side of the room...seemed kind of boring, but whatever. But then the albino Santa called out my name. "Craig Wendel, come forward."

At this point I'm thinking, "Hey buddy, my dad is on the Pastor's Counsel so don't mess with me! Hurry up and find my name and let's get this silly thing over with." For whatever reason, still to this day I have no idea why, but the pasty pontiff couldn't find my name in his book. He looked at me and said, "I never knew you, depart from me."

I thought, "Cool. I can just go sit down and maybe nap for the rest of this boring Sunday." But then the back door burst open and a dude in a full demon outfit and mask screeched a horrendous noise. I spun around and was absolutely terrified. He had real chains hanging from his wrists and feet giving him the appearance of a deranged lunatic that had just escaped. No, let me correct that. He looked like a *demonic,* deranged lunatic that had just escaped from a crack house. I would love to say I ran and got away, but I didn't. I was absolutely frozen in place with a fear that was palpable. The demonic creature lurched forward and snatched me up over his shoulder, which was the trigger for me to go ghetto on his chained up tail. Of course, an 8 year old going ghetto on a full grown man looked more like a fly caught in a spider's web, a whole lot of flailing, with zero success.

The demon man dragged me out of children's church to the sound of 30 kids crying and screaming, pleading for mercy on their souls. The theatrics worked I guess, because we all got saved that day. I would have just hated to be the cleaning crew that had to clean up those thirty little puddles of pee.

Jesus told us to simply remain in the Father's love.[2] It's not about works and doing, but rather loving and being. That day in children's church, a fear of God was put in me that was not healthy or holy. It drove me to the altar time after time. Each time I planted my flag, once again, in the exact same mountain, starting the exact same relationship with Jesus all over again. And it was simply because I was living my life always running from the boogie man. I had become a flagger.

> It's not about works and doing, but rather loving and being.

For decades, I related to God through fearful obedience instead of a loving relationship. Every time I did anything wrong, no matter how small, I was in fear that God was starting the engine on the truck and was waiting to run me over. Now, if you're a good church-goer you might think, "That's awesome! You felt guilt and so you continued to repent and you stayed close to God and stayed out of sin." What you fail to realize, is that going through life this way, as a flagger, focuses your entire life on behavior modification instead of on cultivating a hot, steamy, passionate relationship with Jesus Christ. Every prayer, every spiritual move, is all about you and the condition of your soul.

Church world is chocked full of people who spend most of their spiritual thinking and spiritual actions making sure that their soul is in line. And whether it is or not doesn't matter, they plant the flag again just to be sure. This spiritual self-centeredness nurtures an environment where everyone just sits around singing Kumbaya with no concern for anyone or anything else around them. These flaggers live a life that is constantly soaked in fear instead of living in power, love, and a sound mind.[3]

> These flaggers live a life that is constantly soaked in fear instead of living in power, love, and a sound mind.

The great reformist, Martin Luther, said that living a life this way in constant fear, always hoping we would somehow measure up to the great demands put on us, was a damnable doctrine and that we should avoid it like the plague.[4] Unfortunately, instead of the plague, it appears that the American church as a whole has embraced it more as a motto, which ironically, has made us appear to the common person as a disease infested group of believers. We walk around hoping to infect others with our miserably defeated lifestyle, as opposed to living in confidence and power, which does not infect others. But instead inspires, transforms and impacts society as a whole. Jesus never hinted or insinuated that we become a drifter, repeater, or a flagger. Instead, He said something that was absolutely right-side-up revolutionary.

SERVERS

Jesus, when he walked in the dust, told us what the *next* thing was. He showed us how to never succumb to spiritual boredom and how to never find ourselves sitting in a circle singing Kumbaya with people wearing knee cymbals. He didn't hide it, in fact he didn't even hint at it. Instead, he blurted it out. He modeled it by the way he lived, and then, when he was resurrected, he reiterated the exact same thing.

He told us to serve. At first glance, the idea of serving holds zero grams of glitz or glam that we believe to be reflective of the mountain top experience. We think that each and every so called 'mountain top experience' should be punctuated with flash bulbs, screaming fans, and the tantalizing rhythm of our very own theme music. But when it comes to serving, all we think of is pain, drudgery, and hard work with almost zero return on investment. Serving is the next step down from the peak. Ironically, it's a step down in the time space continuum (I have no idea what that means but it sounds good) but it's a step up, spiritually. The only way to continually go up is through serving. The only way to never get bored or under-whelmed with God, Jesus, or the church world, is through serving others. By helping others get to the top and experience the same summit euphoria that you did, you get the privilege of vicariously experiencing that same freshness that you started with. When we serve others into the Kingdom like this, it invigorates us and motivates us to keep climbing.

> The only way to never get bored or under-whelmed with God, Jesus, or the church world, is through serving others.

Adam, my personal rainforest Sherpa, somehow stumbled upon the secret of finding joy in others finding joy. By him attempting to take me to the top, helping me and cajoling me, it was as if he was climbing the cliff for the first time again through my eyes. He felt the fear and relished in the excitement of a new adventure. If you are wondering what's next on your journey, or maybe you're even a little bit bored with church and the whole following Jesus thing, then I know this book is going to challenge you and help you discover the forgotten excitement and joy that you used to have. By taking a page out of the Sherpa playbook, we are going to discover what it takes to never live another dull day as long as we walk this planet.

SHERPA CHECKLIST

1. In what ways has your walk with Christ become predictable?

2. What things have you added to your walk with Christ in hopes that it would increase your relationship with Him?

3. How many times have you gotten "saved" in an effort to renew your commitment to Christ, hoping that each time it would be a newer and more exciting experience?

4. Why does serving have such a negative connotation to it? Why do we find ourselves shying away from serving yet we seek to be served?

2
THE LEAD

THE BEST WAY TO LEARN any action is to watch someone else do it. Of course it's more fun to watch and learn from other people's mistakes. That's why YouTube is such a smash phenomenon. It gives us the ability to watch other people do things that they were never meant to attempt with dizzying results. Sometimes, someone else's pain can be the best teacher, that's exactly how I learned to use a snow blower.

Growing up in Michigan, snow was a part of life and shoveling was a chore that no one really enjoyed. I was born in 1970, so in my formidable years, there was no such thing as a snow blower, just a shovel and a sore back. So, when they invented a machine that was basically like a lawn mower but for snow, I was intrigued.

I was nine years old and standing outside the church with Christmas morning excitement; prepped, primed, and prepared to watch my first snow blower in action. Brother Bruff had bought himself one of these shiny snow demons and had offered to bring it to church and blow off the sidewalks before service. I had heard this was coming and there I was, standing outside in the cold, waiting to watch and learn how to operate a snow blower. I discovered later that it was Brother Bruff's first time running the machine as well, which always ups the ante a bit.

He managed to blow off half the sidewalk with shear precision and I was in awe at how fast it could clear the sidewalk. But then, just as I was about to retreat back inside to the warmth of the church, the snow blower got clogged. Something had gotten stuck in the intake area and caused the snow blower to stop throwing its beautiful sheets of white powder. Brother Bruff had obviously handled this situation before in some previous alternate universe, because it didn't even seem to faze him. He just left the machine running and bent down to knock the protruding hunk of ice into the machine so that it could be obliterated into powder.

I watched as he knocked the ice into the machine, which happened easier than what he thought. He had used too much force and his hand went into the machine, to which the blades of the snow blower succinctly removed his fingers, turning them into a red cloud of mush that magnificently colored the white front lawn of the church. Nothing says, "welcome to our church" quite like blood, sinew, and randomly strewn fingers. I learned that day by example to never, under any circumstances, stick your hand in a snow blower. That's a good life lesson and I will never forget it because Brother Bruff modeled it for me. You just can't argue with experience. We learn from watching others, and others learn from watching us.

Sherpas don't carry the client to the top, nor do they tell them everything to do. Rather through coaching, encouragement and little climbing tips here and there do the Sherpas model tricks of the trade for the inexperienced climber. I've never climbed Mt. Everest, but I'm guessing that in that environment nobody would argue with a Sherpa guide. If he said attach your rope right 'here,' then you would probably comply without question. Not because the Sherpa is overbearing or threatening, but because they know how to climb the mountain. They've done it before. There would never be an argument on whose way is correct. If the experienced Sherpa did it a certain way then that is the right way, no matter what your mountain climbing guidebook that you bought at the thrift store tells you.

Sherpas are born at an extreme elevation and, unless they move, they live out their entire lives at an elevation that would greatly hinder other races of people on the planet. This high altitude birth has placed things in their DNA that no other people group on the globe has. We will look specifically at this mystery gene in the next chapter, but for now, let me just say that this mystery gene that geneticists have discovered in the Sherpas cause them to be able to perform tasks at extreme elevation that no one else can. While clients are acclimating to the elevation at the base camp, the Sherpas climb to the top of the mountain, stringing safety rope the entire way, laying ladders across crevasses, and strategically placing oxygen bottles at various camps up the mountain. They do all that and then return to the base camp to help their clients achieve the summit that they just left.

Once you've been to the top and planted your flag in the life of Christ, only then does your life description change. It is no longer about you and yours, but now about them and theirs. You become a Spiritual Sherpa, and now to get the most out of life, to experience abundant life[5], you need to serve others by helping them also get to the top. Jesus instructed us in the book of Matthew that if we want to be

> It is no longer about you and yours, but now about them and theirs.

great and enjoy the finer things in the Kingdom, then here on Earth, we have to serve others.[6] If you really want to experience amazing things, have God work amazing things through you, and if you really want to be a big dog in the Kingdom, you have to realize that you get there by serving. Serving is the missing step in modern Christianity. It unlocks a secret passage that allows us to experience a level of excitement and satisfaction that is inaccessible any other way.

Almost every time I talk to others about leading other people up the mountain, or leading them to Jesus, I almost always get the exact same response. The person will give some reason or excuse on how they are not qualified because they don't really know the Bible well enough. They don't even know the ancient 'Roman Road to Salvation.' They get this fear that they will somehow do it wrong and then the person won't really be saved and it will be their fault. After they have a cathartic moment confessing their lack of spiritual acumen, I say something along the lines of, "Okay, never mind that. How about you just tell me what God has done for you? Tell me your story."

SHOW ME YOUR TALE

Sherpas run safety ropes from the base camp, all the way up to the peak of Mt. Everest first. That allows the other neophyte climbers to easily attach their harnesses to the safety line and maintain the right path. These climbers benefit every step of the way from the Sherpa that went before them. It doesn't matter if it is white out conditions, or if the neophyte climber loses his map. You can't get lost when you are hooked onto the tail of the one that climbed before you. Knowing all the nuances of climbing might benefit you while getting to the top, but nothing is going to lead you there more accurately and safely than the line that has already been strung.

You can't get lost when you are hooked onto the tail of the one that climbed before you.

The way we venture through life and eventually come to that spiritual peak of meeting Jesus is a glorious tale. All of us have a different tale to tell. What did you have to wade through or climb over to finally get to the top to meet Christ? What's your story; Molestation, addiction, rape, divorce, gossip, or maybe death by church attendance? No matter how you found your way to the top, your story is guaranteed to be an original, and it's your story that is what will lead the way for someone else to summit the peak where your rope and your life are now securely anchored.

Too often we think that what will help other people is more theology, or maybe a quick crash course in Hebrew or Greek. So we dig down deep in the scriptures and tear out the miniscule details surrounding some other obscure point of view. Truth be told, none of my in-depth teaching or training has ever helped lead someone to the cross. But one thing I have discovered over the years is that God uses our stories over and over again to bring people to the cross.

In the book of Luke there is a story about this guy who was possessed by demons. Not just one or two, but the Bible calls it a legion. In modern day mathematical terms, that's a bunch. So Jesus does his Jesus thing on the guy and kicks all the demons out of him and the man is completely transformed and in his right mind, sitting at the feet of Jesus listening to him teach. Now that's awesome! But when it's time for Jesus to leave, the former-psychopath wants to go with him, and Jesus says, *"No, go back to your family and tell them everything God has done for you."*

I don't know about your church, but the church I grew up in, this guy is so not ready to be sharing Jesus with anybody yet. He must be enrolled in a Sunday School class, get at least one or two seminars under his belt, and then read the entire bible (including Amos and Nahum) cover to cover and have a solid evangelism plan of action in place. He must attend church regularly and sit on one of the first three rows in the auditorium, unless of course he is on the usher team and then he can sit in the special 'reserved usher seats' in the back. Then, after being brought before the church and accepted into the fold, then and only then, should he go share what God did for him.

We are so messed up in the church. We have successfully taken the powerful Gospel narrative (which by the way means "story") and turned it into an impotent structure and form. We have taught people that they need to memorize this form and ritual and that if they follow this formula, they can successfully lead people to Christ. It's comparable to pubescent kids sitting in their first algebra class, sweating bullets that if they forget the formula they will fail. If given a choice, they would just choose not to participate. Sharing Christ is not a formula. Formulas don't love people to Christ. Formulas treat people like common appliances instead of the rare pieces of art that they are.

> We have successfully taken the powerful Gospel narrative and turned it into an impotent structure and form.

When my wife and I moved to the Memphis area to start our church, we didn't know anybody. We did what they call in church planting world, a parachute drop church plant. After a while, we met more and more people and then those people started setting up meetings for me with some of their friends. Through one person to another, I eventually found myself sitting at Starbucks, across the table from a guy that was supposedly interested in becoming part of our church plant.

I knew the guy was squirrelly when he wouldn't even order coffee. I offered to buy it for him but he refused. He was all jumpy and totally thinking about something else, but when you are planting a church and looking for people, you take even the squirrelly ones. In fact, you follow a very strict set of guidelines: If they are breathing, then you want them on the team. This guy was breathing, thus I wanted him. The minute his seat hit the seat he started telling me about how God created man in His image and how man sinned which separated God from man, and on and on the guy droned. I let him walk me all the way through the Old Testament thinking that at any minute he would slow down and ask me how my day was going, or something, but he didn't. As soon as he hit the birth of Jesus I really couldn't take it any longer and leaned forward and said, "Hey man, listen, this is a great lesson, and I'm really loving the story, but I thought we were meeting to talk about my new church plant?"

He never answered or responded. He did, at least, stop talking while I was talking, but as soon as I paused, back into his story we went. He went on for about another fifteen minutes straight and then leaned forward and said, "This is the part of the story where I normally ask if you would like to receive Christ into your heart."

I gave him my best pastoral glare that is normally reserved for the mom with the unruly child in church, and said, "You have got to be kidding me? Seriously? You do realize I'm starting a church, right?"

He replied, "Would you like to accept Christ into your heart today?"

Of course I was in a serious quandary, because I wanted to say no, but what saved person says no to Christ? It's just not going to happen. But if I say yes, then I have to pray to receive Christ again and I just didn't need to do that. So I answered his question the best way I knew how. I stood up and walked out without saying a word.

Needless to say, he never joined our launch team. He became the first breathing person that I didn't want on the team. He was stuck in the formula trap. He had been poorly taught that if he followed this exact same pattern and ritual with me that I'd get saved. To this guy, and a lot of other people in our country, there is a certain formula that one must adhere to if they're going to receive Christ. It has to be done precisely right, and by adopting

> Formulas don't lead people. Stories and relationships lead people.

that thought process, we instill in people that formulas lead people to Christ. Formulas don't lead people. Stories and relationships lead people.

In John Chapter Four there is an amazing story that has become part of Christian folklore, known as "The Woman at the Well." In many regards it is the quintessential story demonstrating how to evangelize a non-believer. In college, I had an entire semester course on evangelism and this story was the main text used for the entire class. From this story we extracted a couple of sure-fire formulas to win hearts over to the side of Jesus Christ. I mean after all, it worked for Jesus. With all the studying and deep research, I think we over looked a huge part of it, because it really wasn't a story that was about a formula, but it was actually a story about a person.

YOUR TALE IS ATTRACTIVE

Every person has a story, and this lady at the well had one also. The Bible tells us that she had been married five times before and now she was shacking up with a guy who she was not married to! Nowadays, unfortunately, our society thinks this is not really a big deal. But in Bible times this was a crazy big deal. If your aunt, sister, or cousin, had been married 5 times and was now living with a guy, even today, we would have a few side comments or off color jokes for them. Now amplify that a few hundred times, and we begin to get a picture of a lady who was ostracized by her community. She was a lady that didn't have a lot of friends and was more than likely disenfranchised by her own peers.[7] Jesus doesn't shy away from her story, but rather digs in and calls attention to it. He could have talked with her and covered all the stuff that He was already planning on saying, and never bring up her past, but He did bring it up. In fact, he made it to where she had to confess it herself. Jesus didn't do this every time somebody was at a spiritual crossroads with Him, but this time He did. He knew that for her well-being, and the well-being of her village, her story needed to surface.

It's hard for us to let our skeletons out of the closet, isn't it? We prefer to leave those things in the dark shadows of our past and never bring them up again. We want people to know us, for who we are right now, today, and I guess there is some validity to that. But it is our past that has made us who we are today. Even the things that we sincerely regret still help form us in some way, and it's this life changing past that we want to hide, that Jesus wants to exploit.

> Even the things that we sincerely regret still help form us in some way.

Jesus excavated this lady's shady past and helped her see that no matter what she had done, He was still the Savior. He was the one that could give her the life she was longing for. Now, to me, the greatest part of this story is not their interaction at the well. I love the part that comes after their conversation.

Once the lady recognizes her past and allows Christ to reconcile her past, her past is no longer a debt, but now an asset; an asset that she uses to transform her entire town. Many of the people in the town started believing in Jesus because the woman said, "He told me everything I ever did!"[8] She already knew what she had done and the life she had lived, but now Jesus brought it into the open, and she realized that her past, her story, her tale, was not something to hide, but actually something to display because it was no longer a present reality, but merely a part of her story that she had been set free and delivered from.

Now this insecure, fear filled woman is using the very thing that used to cripple her, as a tool to bring others closer to Christ, and it worked. It wasn't a formula, or a certain tactical maneuver, but rather a woman telling how her story and His story merged into *the* story. Then our next reference point in this story is where we hear the people of the village say, *"Now we believe, not just because of what you told us, but because we have heard Him ourselves. Now we know that He is indeed the Savior of the world."*[9]

Her story worked. It didn't save the others, but it led them to where they needed to be. The tale of her life was a safety line through all the white noise and snowstorms of public opinion, trite formulas, and quick fix schemes. It guided them to the top of the mountain where they could meet Jesus for themselves. Her story made the difference, and our stories do too.

> Her life was a safety line through all the white noise and snow-storms of public opinion.

Usually, the things from our past that we are still trying to hide, are the things that we are still trying to come to grips with, and are the very things we haven't fully accepted Christ's forgiveness or direction for. Your tale, no matter how difficult it was for you to navigate, is not to be left in the dark. Many of the difficult situations from our past, where pain and discomfort were involved, require a time of healing, and that healing should and must come first. There's nothing worse than having a stranger tromp through the delicate miseries of a recent pain only to make you re-live the anguish that you were working so hard to nurture back to health. But once those individual pieces to our story have found healing and forgiveness in Christ, then we need to pull them out of hiding and use them to lead others in the right direction.

PUT YOUR TALE ON DISPLAY

Instead of trying to hide our past failures and issues, we should take a page from the playbook of David in the Bible. One of the most famous encounters of David is when he fought Goliath the giant. It's a story that's been taught and dissected so many times in church world, that I even hesitate to mention it, but too often the story ends with the killing of the giant. That's a great ending, but an even better ending is seeing what David did with the giant's head.

After David killed Goliath, he cut off the giant's head and took it to Jerusalem.[10] The battle took place in an area called Socoth,[11] so that means David carried Goliath's bloody head 41 miles! I wonder how many times during that journey that David got to testify about God's victory? I wonder how many times he had the opportunity to point someone else to the greatness of God by pulling the bloody head from his gunnysack and holding it up high, praising God for the victory over the biggest thing he ever had to face in his life. Then, encouraging the bystanders by letting them know that whatever they are going through, no matter how big the problem, issue, or giant appears to be, if you will just trust God, then He will make you victorious.

> If you will just trust God, then He will make you victorious.

SHERPA CHECKLIST

1. How much of your Christian, prayer, and bible study life is focused on yourself and your own issues?

2. How different would your life be if you shifted your spiritual focus to others?

3. Do you think serving could be a missing step in modern Christianity?

4. Do you think too much emphasis is put on serving others or not enough?

5. How often do you use your ugly past as an attractant to show others the way to the top of the mountain?

3

THE GEAR

HERE, IN THE STATES, THE name 'Sherpa' is known more as a brand name rather than a people group. A quick Google search will help you find a Sherpa pet carrier, a Sherpa voice controlled assistant, and even a durable Sherpa jacket with undies to match. However, even Google can't explain why the Sherpa people are so extraordinary at high elevations. For many years, geneticists thought that maybe it was due to a high red blood cell count, since it is the red blood cells that transport oxygen to the different parts of the body. But after further research, they discovered that the Sherpas actually have less red blood cells than other populations that are well adapted to high altitude living such as the Quechuans of Peru. In fact, Sherpas red blood cell count is so low that if they were at sea level they would be classified as anemic. They have discovered that Sherpas do have wider blood vessels, thus a greater quantity of blood is circulated at once. Most importantly, they have inherited a unique dominant genetic trait that improves their hemoglobin saturation, which allows their red blood cells to soak up more oxygen.[12]

In other words, the Sherpas were made that way. God formed them as a unique group of people with unique skills that meet the unique need of where they live. It

> We too were created with a unique set of skills and gifts that meet the needs of our unique environment.

was part of the great deity's master design, and like the Sherpas, we too were created with a unique set of skills and gifts that meet the needs of our unique environment.

Look at how the Apostle Paul says it in 1 Corinthians 12:7. *"Each person is given something to do that shows who God is: Everyone gets in on it, everyone benefits. All kinds of things are handed out by the Spirit, and to all kinds of people!"*[13] I love how he says '*everyone*.' I think what he means by this is: Everyone. Every single one of us has something special inside of us that has a special purpose and that purpose is to show other people who God is.

Jesus knew that if the responsibility was really going to be on us to advance the kingdom of God and bring people up the mountain to meet the Savior, then we were going to need some help, and Jesus told us that helper was coming. He said it this way, *"But the Helper, the Holy Spirit, whom the Father will send in my name, he will teach you all things and bring to your remembrance all that I have said to you."*[14]

Some people flip out at the mention of the Holy Spirit. They view Him a lot like crazy Uncle Eddie. Everybody has a crazy Uncle in the family, and it's just easier if we don't talk about him. But the Holy Spirit is not crazy or weird. Unfortunately, people have portrayed Him as such to the general population through several demonstrative acts that freak people out. In some cases, the stranger the occurrence the more it's identified with the Holy Spirit; Which leads people to believe that the Holy Spirit is just going to take over their body and put them in some sort of trance or coma, all while causing them to gyrate and twitch, in comparison to what's best described as Elvis having a seizure.

The Holy Spirit is the third person of the Trinity. I don't really want to debate whether or not you think the Holy Spirit is real, or whether

He still does what He used to do, or any of that stuff.[15] Honestly, I could not imagine going through life without the Holy Spirit walking with me every step of the way. Jesus told us that the Holy Spirit would come and give us gifts to use while He [Jesus] was away and that the Holy Spirit would help us in times of need. I don't know about you, but I want and need all the help I can get. I can tell you instance after instance in my life where the Holy Spirit has prompted me, guided me, or helped me in various ways. He is absolutely amazing, and no, none of those times involved my body twitching, gyrating, convulsing, dancing, sweating, or handling any snakes. I would however, gyrate, dance, and convulse if I saw a snake. Those things creep me out!

GUARANTEE

The Holy Spirit is the one who endows us with gifts, but He is also the guarantee that Christ is actually coming back for us. In John chapter 14, we read what is sort of like the last will and testament of Jesus. He is telling his disciples that He's going away, and they can't come where He's going, but while He's gone He's going to send His partner, the Holy Spirit, to be with them to inspire them and give them endurance to survive life in His absence.

In Ephesians it says that we are *"sealed with the promise of the Holy Spirit, who is the guarantee of our inheritance..."*[16] Since the New Testament was written in colorful Koine Greek, it sometimes helps to look at the meaning of the Greek word in depth and not just rely on the flat words of the English language. Here in this verse the Apostle Paul says that the Holy Spirit is our Guarantee. The Greek word for Guarantee is *arrabōn,* which has also been used when referring to an engagement ring.

When Patti and I were dating, she lived in Huntsville, AL and I was going to college just outside of Chattanooga, TN. I would get out of class on Friday and leave immediately to make the three hour drive to see my sweetheart and spend the weekend with her. Of course, that meant

The Holy Spirit guarantees that Christ will return for us.

she was left unattended without proper boyfriend supervision for approximately 5 days. That didn't bother me too bad since I was not just any boyfriend I was a bonafide fiancée! I had given her a guarantee that I was coming back. Looking back now, it wasn't much of a guarantee, but back then it was a huge rock that obviously stopped traffic and even caused the Hubble Telescope to become out of focus. I gave her my very best and *that best* did a couple of things. It showed Patti that I was coming back for her. After all, it's not like it was just a cheap string of Mardi Gras beads that I threw to every good looking girl that crossed my path. It was a diamond ring! Secondly, it showed everybody else that she was taken. She was no longer on the market. The Holy Spirit guarantees that Christ will return for us. He is the engagement ring as it were, to the ultimate wedding between Christ and his bride, the Church.

TOOLS OF THE TRADE

The Holy Spirit gives us the right stuff to get up the mountain. He equips us with what we need to not only get ourselves to the top, but others as well. Just as the Sherpas use their unique genetic make up to prepare the mountain for novice climbers to reach the top, so the Holy Spirit equips us to help and serve others in a way that propels them to the pinnacle of their spiritual journey. The gifts of the Holy Spirit are meant to be tools to help and serve others.

One of my hobbies is woodworking. I tried golf like all the other pastors I know, but every time I played, I found myself cussing like a sailor and having a strong desire to drink like one too. So, in the best interest of my personal walk with Jesus, I found it was best to never set foot on a golf course again. Even to this day, when I drive by a golf course I feel the resurgence to utter things that a pastor just ought not to say. So I switched to woodworking, it's safer.

I have a shop full of fun power tools. If you can plug it in and it cuts, grinds, drills, or sands, I think I have it. There is not much I can't do or build with the tools I have. I am fully equipped to build whatever my wife has a hankering for, but nothing gets built, fixed, or repaired if I keep all the tools in their place. I can brag about the tools to all my friends and talk about how awesome they are and how I have a tool for every situation, but all of that is really just lip service. Nothing ever comes of it unless I actually pull the tools out and use them.

The Holy Spirit equips us with usable gifts that are meant to be used with the purpose of leading people up the mountain and showing them who God is. Now, you can join the group of people that say, "Well that's just not for me" if you want to, but the Bible did say that everyone gets in on it and I'm pretty sure you fit in the category of everyone.

> The Holy Spirit equips us with usable gifts that are meant to be used.

In 1 Corinthians, the Apostle Paul lists several gifts of the Holy Spirit. This is not the only listing of various gifts, but it's a pretty good one. At the end of the list he said, *"All these* [gifts] *are empowered by one and the same Spirit, who apportions to each one individually as he wills."*[17]

Now, I was raised in a denomination that believed the only way you could have the Holy Spirit was if you had the gift of speaking in tongues. If marijuana is the 'gateway drug' to all other drugs, then speaking in tongues was the 'gateway gift' that lead to all the others. You had to speak in tongues to prove that you had the Holy Spirit in your life. I respect that, but I don't read that. The Holy Spirit gives to each one the gift that he wants to, or in other words, the Holy Spirit gives different gifts to different people to meet the unique needs of the people that we are interacting with. The goal is not to show off a gift, but rather to put a gift or tool in your toolbox that you can use to

> If marijuana is the 'gateway drug' to all other drugs, then speaking in tongues was the 'gateway gift' that lead to all the others.

meet the unique needs of the people in the hostile cultural environment that we live in.

If it weren't for the promptings and direction of the Holy Spirit, I think I'd be dead, or worse. This past summer, I was in the parking lot of our church pulling weeds in between the cement curb and the asphalt parking lot. It's an older building and a much older parking lot, so the weeds are a constant issue. I was going along pulling weeds and picking up little pieces of trash, not really thinking about anything in particular. About ten feet down was a small piece of wood, maybe six inches square, leaning up against the curb. Of course, I thought absolutely nothing of it since our parking lot is a magnet for many strange things, all of them much stranger than a piece of wood. As I got about six feet from it, I heard the Holy Spirit say, "Be careful, there's a snake under there." This is of course ludicrous, since no snake would be stupid enough to hang out in a parking lot, in Mississippi, in the middle of summer; Way too hot for that. I kept weeding and moving closer to the wood. When I was right next to it I heard the Holy Spirit again say, "Be careful there's a snake under there."

I have been accused of being a lot of things, but smart and brilliant are never on the list. With all the confidence of a man wearing a straight jacket locked in a padded room, I literally laughed out loud and said back to the Holy Spirit in my best Balaam impersonation, "No, there's not!" and proceeded to flip the board back onto the asphalt to reveal a Copperhead snake coiled up, chilling in the shade of the board. He didn't like being brought into the bright southern sun, so he jerked up at the exact same moment that I jumped up and began gyrating, dancing, and screaming all over the church parking lot. Of course, seeing me dance in the parking lot was probably not good for attendance, but some things you just can't help. The Holy Spirit speaks, guides, and directs us if we will just listen and be attuned to His presence.

> The Holy Spirit speaks, guides, and directs us if we will just listen.

Many times, people view the workings of the Holy Spirit as something that is done *to* us instead of a supernatural power that works *through* us. Being raised in a very demonstrative church, the Holy Spirit was always portrayed as this mystical force that would do something to us. But when you start looking at the third person of the Trinity in the New Testament, we discover that He might very well do things *to* us, but His primary function is to do things *through* us. Your car might make you feel warm and safe on a cold winter's night, but that is not the primary function of the car. Its primary function is to transport you from one location to the next. Walking with the Holy Spirit has amazing benefits, like a supernatural peace that passes all understanding, but the lead role of the Holy Spirit is to flow through us to show others who God is.

The Holy Spirit encourages us to keep climbing, and constantly reminds us that Jesus really is coming back for us. Plus, on top of that, He equips us with the gifts, or gear, that we need to make the climb and take as many people with us as possible. If the gifts of the Spirit are mostly externally witnessed, the fruits of the spirit are an internal formation. We need the gifts to get stuff done, but we need the fruit to support the gifts and make sure they are used appropriately and accurately.

> The fruits of the spirit are an internal formation.

FRUITS

The fruits of the spirit that are found in the book of Galatians give us a great list to look at and draw from.[18] The verse informs us that the fruits of the spirit are: love, joy, peace, patience, kindness, goodness, faithfulness, gentleness, and self-control. These internal traits help keep the external gifts in order. When someone only focuses on the external gifts of the spirit without nurturing and growing the internal fruits, they end up misusing their gifts and end up knocking people off the mountain. They cause more harm than good.

Sebastian had been coming to church for a few months and every time he came he made sweet little old church ladies scamper to the safety of their favorite pew. They would hold their hankies up to their mouths and slowly wag their head back and forth in disgust. Now and then, they might whisper the infamous church line, "Bless his heart." All the while looking down at him in fear, trepidation, and a tad bit of, "I'm so glad I'm not like him." Sebastian was 17 years old and he was about as lost as one could be. No family, not many friends and nobody really knew where he lived. He always looked disheveled and had a certain funk to him that you would usually only smell at Pink Floyd concerts. He had several tattoos, but that wasn't the head turner. Part of what caused people to gasp was his multiple piercings. He looked like he'd fallen face first into my grandfather's tackle box; hooks, clips, spikes, feathers, and anything else he could find laying around. His face alone could set off a metal detector 20 yards away, but even with all that, it was still not the head turner. The real show stopper was both of his collarbones. They were pierced, not once or twice, but numerous times. From shoulder to neck were safety pins, which he proudly showed off by almost always wearing a tank top. These were not professionally done piercings either, they were homemade, and each and every puncture on his collarbone was infected, red, puffy and painful to even look at. But he came to church.

Over the course of a few months I got to know him and was able to build a little bit of a rapport with him. He was a hurting kid, lost in life and looking for answers. He didn't believe in God but he thought he would check church out for a while to see if any of it could answer some of his life questions. I knew that if he just kept coming and kept seeking God that eventually he would make it to the top of the mountain and meet Jesus. I looked forward to seeing him every Sunday.

George was a great guy at the church. He was older than the majority of people there and had a lot of respect from the congregation. He loved God with all his heart and had committed his life to serving the Lord all the time. George was part of a lot of different ministries and one of them was the prayer ministry at the church. George had several various gifts from the Holy Spirit; in fact, he would probably argue that he had them all. If a gift was needed he was like Quick Draw McGraw. He was always the first one with a prayer, a word of encouragement, or a teaching lesson. George had gifts, and the infamous Sunday when Sebastian decided to climb the mountain and meet Jesus, George was there to bring the full weight of his gifts to bear on the problem at hand.

The Senior Pastor gave an inspiring message and then opened the altars for people to come and pray. Sebastian stood up and began walking down front. There was a collective gasp as he was spotted by the head-waggers, but Sebastian didn't really seem to care. He was focused on reaching the top of the mountain that day, and finally getting his life questions answered. He walked right up to George and said, "I think I need Jesus, will you pray for me?"

George looked at him, and in a matter of fact tone said, "I'll pray for you when you take all those piercings out."

Sebastian lowered his head, turned around, and walked out. George doesn't minister on the prayer team anymore. Now, you might think that story is extreme, and maybe it is, but I don't think so. Unfortunately, events like that happen all the time in church world. People receive gifts from the Holy Spirit, yet fail to cultivate the internal fruit of

He lacked the internal fruit to support and perpetuate the outward gifts of the Holy Spirit.

the Holy Spirit which keeps the gifts in check and in balance. George might have had numerous gifts, but he lacked the internal fruit to support and perpetuate the outward gifts of the Holy Spirit. When we find ourselves in that situation, we end up doing more harm than good for the Kingdom. We wildly flail our gifts around, while knocking numerous people off the mountain that they were climbing.

Just like fruit on a tree, the fruit of the Spirit must be patiently grown and nurtured. You never hear an apple tree straining to pop out an apple, do you? The tree doesn't grunt and groan until each little apple is somehow birthed onto its branches. It's a process. A gift is given, but fruit is grown. Odds are the husband with anger issues who got saved a week ago is still going to have a struggle with his anger until the full fruits of kindness and gentleness blossom and grow in his heart. The single mom with 3 kids (all under the age of ten) who keep her running from one thing to the next, and has only been walking with the Lord for a year, still needs time for peace and patience to grow. Then, there is the teenager who has an extremely low self-esteem and struggles with self-inflicted pain, like cutting. They all decide to give Jesus a try and they become overwhelmed with His grace and mercy, and therefore, commit their lives to follow Him. Yes, they get on the right path, but that doesn't mean that they have a full orchard of love-fruit growing in them yet. It's still a process no matter who you are or where you come from, and each of us needs to focus on the internal growth of the fruit, not just the exciting and sometimes demonstrative gifts.

The Sherpa's mystery gene allows them to do incredible feats of heroism every single day in some of the most hostile environments on the planet. Novice climbers watch them carry heavy loads and endure sub-zero temperatures, all while simultaneously caring for the weakest and least experienced climbers among them. The Holy Spirit that resides in us is that supernatural force that encourages, equips, and develops us into spiritual guides on the mountain of the Lord. Each of us is gifted in a unique way to meet the unique challenges of our daily lives, with a commission to get as many people to the top as possible.

> Each of us is gifted in a unique way to meet the unique challenges of our daily lives

SHERPA CHECKLIST

1. How do you allow the Holy Spirit to operate in your life?

2. What tools have you discovered that the Holy Spirit has put in you?

3. What do you think about the Holy Spirit doing things through you and not just to you?

4. Do the fruits of the Spirit drive the gifts of the Spirit in your life, or do the gifts drive the fruit?

4

PAIN AND DISCOMFORT

It is not a specific need that drives us to invent something; it's a lack of comfort.

THERE IS AN OLD ADAGE that says, "Necessity is the mother of invention." I disagree. In our country it is not a specific need that drives us to invent something; it's a lack of comfort. Anywhere where we find pain, anxiety, a long line, or a hard surface, we grow a desire to alleviate the world from such discomfort.

When Patti and I lived in Honduras there was a lot to get used to. We left all the comforts of home and moved to a rain forest village up the mountain where we were the only ones who spoke English. Ironically, we also spoke very poor Spanish. Nothing came easily there. Everything was laborious; from washing clothes on a washboard to having to burn our own used toilet paper. Nothing says love like burning your spouse's booty tissue for them. We were blessed because unlike everyone else in the village who lived in mud huts with thatched roofs, Patti and I lived in a luxurious cement block home that measured a whopping 15x30 feet. We did have a bed, which was fairly comfortable, except for the fact that when the sun goes down the Central American Cockroaches come out.[19] It's just not that comfortable to be lying there and having bugs crawl up and down your body and face, it's a bit unnerving to say the least.

One night, a particularly large cockroach climbed up my face and started into my nose. I'm sure this probably wouldn't have bothered you much, and you would have just slept right through it, but for me it rattled my cage. I snatched the bug up and flung it across the room in a mix of panic, fear, and joy that at least it wasn't a snake. In the morning I was still a bit beside myself and wanted to share my misery with my wife, so I asked her, "Hey babe, how'd you sleep last night?"

To which she replied, "Oh, fine. I did have this cockroach start to climb in my ear though."

"Really! What did you do?"

"Well, he only made it half way into my ear so I just grabbed the back of him, pulled him out, and then squeezed him until I heard him pop. Then I just went back to sleep."

"Until I heard him pop." Sexier words have never been spoken. I knew at that moment that I married the greatest woman on the planet, and I also knew right then that I had to invent something to keep the bugs off of us at night. The discomfort of that night drove me to hunt, find and discover some netting that became known as our "candy coated shell." I attached it to the rafters and then let it hang down over the bed and then I tucked it securely under the mattress forming a bug free tent. It kept the bugs off, but not the lizards; but that's another story. It was the *discomfort* of the cockroach caravan, not *necessity*, which drove me to be an inventor.

Famed mountaineer Dave Hahn said, "On the Mountain, being uncomfortable is not extra credit, it's just the entrance fee." He should know since he has summited Mt. Everest more than any other non-Sherpa to date. Mt. Everest is a merciless place where people die from frostbite, exposure, snow blindness and a myriad of other ailments. Atop the tallest peak on the planet, comfort is not even a consideration.

Being uncomfortable is not extra credit, it's just the entrance fee.

But when it comes to Christianity, it appears to be one of the leading causes of conversions. Now it might not be the number one thing that causes people to accept Christ, but I would venture a guess and say that it's in the top five.

NOT ABOUT COMFORT

People usually get so fed up with their life and the way things are going, that they venture into church and hear a minister say, in some form or fashion, that if they will accept Jesus into their hearts then everything will be rainbows and unicorns from then on. That's like saying all the traffic lights on the way to work will always be green, never red; maybe an occasional yellow, but never red. Or, their spouse will fall madly in love with them again and their children will love and respect them and participate in first time obedience to the parent's every whim and command. Now maybe I'm exaggerating a little bit, but the truth still remains somewhere in there.

We do a great job of convincing people that their lives will be so much better when they are walking with Jesus. We tell them about the power of the resurrection of Jesus, and the gift of healing, and how they can, by faith, tell mountains to move. But it's almost as if we get people to jump on the boat, while leading them to believe the Christian life is a pleasure cruise, when really, it's a battleship headed into unfriendly waters. Once the bombs start bursting in air, and family members start shunning us, then we feel like we have been sold a bill of goods.

Yes, it's true, there are wonderful blessings in the Bible, and I could not imagine living one

Life *in* God is far superior to life *outside* of God.

single day without the hand of God in my life. I don't think I have enough time left on the planet to count the blessings that He has given me. but just because it is so fabulous does not mean that no pain or discomfort will ever abound. The Bible is clear on this and teaches the same thing that we all experience, but for some reason, we normally don't teach it as clearly as the Bible does. The Bible says things about us sharing in His sufferings, and taking up our cross. It even says in Galatians[20] that we are crucified with Christ! Now what's all that about? That sounds absolutely painful!

The truth of the matter is that once we step into a relationship with Jesus Christ there are stupendous benefits, but there is also no standing promise that nothing will ever go wrong. Pain is inevitable, whether it's from a financial failure, a broken home, or the death of a loved one; pain is coming to your home. It's not *whether* or not it arrives, but rather, how we handle it once it *does* arrive. Still, so many people across our nation continue to accept Christ day after day, believing that once they say a prayer and start a relationship with this mystical being called Christ, all their problems will disappear as quickly as a free doughnut display at a Weight Watchers convention.

Then, the proverbial Monday morning appears, and we wake up only to discover that our spouse still has stinky breath, the dog vomited all over our great grandmothers comforter, the kids all have a fever, and the electricity was turned off because somebody forgot to pay the power bill. We lay there trying to think of what to do next and the only thing we can come up with is what has been modeled and handed down to us through the annals of time: Fake it. It's simple and easy; nobody can really know the truth. After all, we just accepted Christ into our hearts; that means everything should be fine and we will have no issues or problems. If people knew that we were saved, and still had problems, they might begin to wonder if we were really saved to begin with. Faking it is definitely a viable option.

WHEN IN DOUBT, FAKE IT

I grew up with some of the best fakers in the business. Then, after I got a little older and had issues of my own, I discovered a whole new level of fakers. They're the ones that can have their lives crumbling around them and they are still waxing and coating everything in such a thick layer of spiritual idioms that you're not really sure if their dog just died or they just returned from the Mount of Transfiguration. Every sentence starts and ends with hallelujah, or praise Jesus. It's as if there is a major disconnect between their pain and their Savior, and that the two cannot coexist, yet Jesus coexisted with pain and discomfort in every way.

We only focus on the obvious cultural victories in the Bible; I say it that way because what appears to be a failure on the surface could very well be a victory in the eyes of God. The eleventh chapter of Hebrews is known as the chapter of faith. The writer of Hebrews lists all these amazing people that have done amazing things in the Kingdom of God. He starts by talking about the faith of Abel and moves on to Abraham, Isaac, Moses, and even fits in the courageous acts of Rahab the Jericho hooker turned spy. The list goes on and on to mention people that we would all emulate and hope to be like under pressure. Their acts of greatness are listed in the greatest book on the globe.

Then the author seems to shift gears, yet he doesn't. He seems to change topics, but he doesn't. In the same flow of listing great men and women of faith he says this: *"But others were tortured, refusing to turn from God in order to be set free. They placed their hope in a better life after the resurrection. Some were jeered at, and their backs were cut open with whips. Others were chained in prisons. Some died by stoning, some were sawed in half, and others were killed with the sword. Some went about wearing skins of sheep and goats, destitute and oppressed and mistreated."*[21]

No matter how bad my day might be going, it's always better than being sawn in half. These people served Christ faithfully through some of the most horrific trials, and they are listed in the chapter of faith right alongside Moses, Samson and King David. They didn't walk away from their faith because they were broke, busted, or disgusted;

> Their economic status, relational status, and health status did not determine their spiritual status.

they recognized that their level of comfort was not in direct proportion to their level of Christianity. They didn't question if Jesus loved them because they had to wear goat or sheepskins instead of a nice cotton polyester blend. Their economic status, relational status, and health status did not determine their spiritual status. We tend to think that they are all interwoven.

If our social status or relational merit goes down, then obviously we have done something wrong for God to punish us. If we bounce a check and find ourselves behind financially then obviously God is no longer pleased with us, and if the report comes back from the doctor announcing cancer, then there is obviously hidden sin in our lives. Too often we use outward natural factors to determine inward spiritual substance because we never consider that God would be okay with us being uncomfortable. Comfort in Christianity is not just an option; we've made it a commodity. So we find ourselves in this place of limbo where we have issues in our lives that cause us discomfort, but nobody else in Christendom seems to have issues, so we fake it and hope nobody finds out the truth. Or, we can recognize and align ourselves to His agony, so that our ailment might be alleviated.

In the last few chapters, we have been talking about taking other people up the mountain to meet Christ, so they too can plant the flag at the pinnacle of their spiritual pursuits. But the truth of the matter is few people do this. According to a recent survey[22] people who claim to have a close walk with Jesus Christ have fewer than six spiritual conversations a year with those outside the church. The number goes down when you consider how many of those conversations lead to conversions, and the majority of church goers said that they rarely or never engage in spiritual conversations with those outside the church. I'm sure part of this lack of evangelistic vigor goes back to the fear of not leading someone to the Lord properly while following a predetermined path that was taught and modeled. But the other factor is our own internal struggle.

SHERPA CHECKLIST

1. Do you allow the level of comfort in your life to be the barometer of the quality of your relationship with Christ?

2. How often do you use your circumstances to determine the strength of your Christian walk?

5

INSECURITIES

We find ourselves operating out of insecurity instead of stepping into the security of who God created us to be.

WE HAVE ISSUES. WE ALL have issues. Maxwell Maltz, author of the book *Psycho-Cybernetics*, estimates that approximately 95% of people in our society have a strong sense of inadequacy. In down to earth terms, that means that about 95% of us are insecure. There are areas of our life where we find ourselves operating out of insecurity instead of stepping into the security of who God created us to be. Each of our lives contains innumerable categories and sections. We are totally secure and comfortable operating in some of them, but then there are others that when we step into them, we get 'that feeling' similar to when a lizard craws up your pant leg and you can't decide whether to do the dance of lunacy or just run in sheer terror.

For you, maybe it's finances or relationships. Maybe you're good with relationships until it comes to certain family members. You can pick your category, but the truth of the matter is each and every one of us has an area, or multiple areas, that we are insecure in; it's this insecurity that hinders us from moving forward in confidence, thus helping others reach their potential and spiritual peak.

Many times we fail to realize our insecurities because we think that insecurities have certain well-defined and narrow characteristics or behavior. The truth of the matter is, insecurities reveal themselves in multiple behaviors or characteristics, and if we think it is only one way then we will continually live in a state of mind that we just don't have to live in.

BLIND ARROGANCE

One of the behaviors that, at first glance, doesn't appear to have anything to do with insecurity is arrogance. People who are that abrasive and aggressive seem to have it all together, so much so, that they become pushy and even braggadocious about things which is actually something that a typical insecure person would never see themselves doing.

This is that guy who has to brag about *everything*. He is always telling everyone what he is driving, what brand he is wearing, and how much his sunglasses cost. He wants you to be acutely aware of the fact that he has a home in the States and a lovely Chateau in some country that you can't even pronounce. His constant bragging and abrasive manner makes you think that he is a jerk or something worse. Although this might be true, he is more than likely insecure. His constant bragging and forwardness is his vain attempt at making you think he is better and more well off than he knows he is.

In 1999 I resigned my job as a Youth Pastor in Alabama in order to move to Florida. I didn't have a job or another place to go, but that's what I felt God telling me to do, so I did. During that time, one of the jobs I landed to feed my family was flipping burgers at an outdoor grill at a country club in Naples, Florida. One day while I was working the grill, a large party of about twenty men walked up together after playing a round of golf. They all ordered burgers and beer. They began talking and laughing and have a good time. It didn't take long to figure out who was the leader of this party. It was the guy that paid for everyone's food and drinks and made sure everyone knew that he had done it. I then watched as he went around from one pocket of men to the next letting them know how awesome he was and how well off he was.

After several moments, he had moved to the edge of the fray and ended up standing right next to me at the grill, when one of his friends walked up and said, "Hey man, how are you doing?" To which the party leader replied in a boisterous tone, "Man I'm great, couldn't be better!" The other guy was undeterred by his bravado and said, "No seriously, cut the crap. How are you really doing?" The party leader transformed almost immediately. He slumped his shoulders, hung his head and said, "I don't know what I'm doing. My wife left me a few weeks ago, my kids won't talk to me, and now it looks like I'm going to have to file bankruptcy." This guy may have appeared to be arrogant and abrasive, but in all actuality he was so insecure in so many areas, that he was working overtime just to keep up the facade.

COMPETITIVE CAMOUFLAGE

Of course it's not just people's arrogance that hides and camouflages people's insecurities; sometimes it's overtly competitive attitudes as well. Now just to be clear, I am not saying that being competitive is a rouge path of destruction. In fact, I believe that if you are going to be on the ball field or any other sports field, you *should* be competitive. I do not subscribe to the practice or belief that everybody should get a trophy. Nope, winners should get trophies, and losers should not.

When my son played T-Ball, I watched as moms would hang on the fence like spider monkeys, yelling and screaming at their sons as well as the umpire. The score would be in the neighborhood of 86 to 45 and every time the ball was whacked off the tee, all the boys in the field would chase after it, looking more like moths trying to mate than a competitive team of ball players, but the moms didn't care. They screamed and shouted and freaked out like it was tied up in the fourth extra inning.

People who are hyper-competitive are always trying to prove to themselves and to others that they are winners and that their insecurities are not nearly as pronounced as they actually are.

THE KING OF INSECURITY

The emotional behaviors that are most associated with insecure people are being overtly shy and backwards and those who live with specific anxiety. Have you ever been in a conversation and the person you were talking to is constantly worrying about what somebody else said or thought about them? They are constantly trolling social media for what others have posted or commented about them with a lingering fear, because after all, they must please people.

For a long time this was one of my biggest insecurities. I wanted to please anybody and everybody. Of course, as a pastor I learned

> We feel the pressure to please others because we are insecure in who we are.

very quickly that it's not only impossible to please everybody, but I can't be productive and please everybody. I had to learn the art of saying no. People who struggle in this area have a hard time computing the fact that you can say no to someone and still remain their friend. But, since we are loaded down with various insecurities, we feel the pressure to please others because we are insecure in who we are.

Then there are the critical ones; the people who are critical about anything and everything. They criticize others by tearing them down and belittling them in order to make themselves feel better. Most of the time, when I see or hear someone who is critical and nitpicks others, that person is very insecure about himself or herself.

Sherpas know their role on the mountain. They don't have time or energy to waste on things like insecurity. If they were insecure then they would remain at the base camp among the baggage and equipment, trying to make sure They don't have time or energy to waste on things like insecurity. they had everything they needed, as well as the skills it takes to climb the mountain. They might criticize others for their gear or climbing skills, or maybe they would stand around and brag about stories from the past, aggrandizing themselves and their small feats of bravery. Perhaps they would engage in trite competitions to show off various skills, once again trying to prove to themselves and to others that they have what it takes. They might do all those things, but the one thing that never climbs a mountain is insecurity, and one thing that always takes our focus off of Christ and helping others is our own insecurities.

When I search the Bible, I don't think I could find a better example of an insecure person than King Saul. Of course, before he was king he was a farmer and the son of a farmer. He is a young man in the smallest tribe in all of Israel and his clan or family is the smallest family unit in the smallest tribe in one of the smallest countries in the world. Saul knows it, and because of that he thinks and feels that everyone else knows it too. I would highly recommend you take the time to read through the book of 1 Samuel, and as you do, pay special attention to all of Saul's key decision making moments, and I think you'll see that every time he had a choice to make, he chose to operate out of his insecurity instead of his calling.

The first time we see Saul is in chapter 1 Samuel 9. His dad lost some donkeys and sent Saul out to find them. Saul, through a series of events, decides to go meet Samuel, the prophet, to see if he can give them some information on where their donkeys might be. What Saul did not know was that the day before, God had visited Samuel and told him that Saul was coming to meet him, and that Saul was God's choice to be the very first king of Israel.

God chose Saul. Samuel didn't choose Saul, and Saul didn't choose to be king. It was God's choice. God chose Saul with the foreknowledge that Saul could overcome his insecurities and be a great king, as long as

God chose Saul with the fore-knowledge that Saul could overcome his insecurities and be a great king.

he listened to the voice of the Lord and not the apprehensive voice in his heart. Saul is a great example of someone who missed opportunity after opportunity to help people and make a difference in the world because he was so focused on his own issues and insecurities. The way Saul was raised and the things that happened to him became the things that piloted his life. Likewise, the way we have been raised and the things that have happened to us have set the course for our lives. That's not an excuse, it's an observation, and if we will make that observation, recognize it and then turn to God in those areas, then He can use us in crazy awesome ways to impact other people's lives. Saul never recognized it and ended up acting out of his insecurity instead of out of his calling.

When Samuel finally meets Saul, their first verbal exchange sets the tone for the rest of Saul's life. Samuel basically tells Saul that he is amazing.[23] Not only is he good looking, we find out that the bible calls Saul the most handsome man in all of Israel; now that's bragging rights! Samuel tells Saul that he is great looking on the outside, and that he has wonderful gifts, skills, and talents on the inside, and on top of all that, the entire country is looking to him for help and direction. Saul's response is priceless.

Saul answered, "But am I not a Benjamite, from the smallest tribe of Israel, and is not my clan the least of all the clans of the tribe of Benjamin? Why do you say such a thing to me?"

Saul, talking to the prophet of the Lord said, "Yeah, I hear you but obviously you don't know me, because I'm the least of the least of the least. You're saying all these wonderful things but what you're saying is not lining up with what I'm experiencing." Have you ever struggled like that before? You hear God or sense God saying things to you, calling you to do amazing things, or to help or serve someone else, but what we are hearing does not line up with what we are experiencing. You read in the Bible where God tells us that He has set us apart[24] and we think, "Yeah, I hear you, but it seems like you have set me apart to be the poster child for the guy with the most issues. I'm on my fifth marriage; I have step kids, step grand kids, stepparents, and even step-in-laws. I have more steps in my family than the Empire State building! So sure, I can see that you set me apart, but based on what I'm experiencing I don't think I like this kind of 'set apart.'"

Weeks later, Samuel calls the entire country together for the first ever coronation service for their new King. Saul knew he was going to be king, and Samuel knew he was going to be king. At this point it was not a surprise to either of them, but when Saul's tribe was called forward, and then Saul's family was called forward, they called for Saul to step forward and he was not there.

But when they looked for him, he had disappeared! So they asked the Lord, "Where is he?" And the Lord replied, "He is hiding among the baggage."[25]

Saul was so insecure in who he was that he found more comfort hiding amongst his own baggage and issues than stepping into what God called him to become. Saul continually chose to remain in his baggage then to step into the freedom and calling that God had established for him.

EXTRA BAGGAGE

I talk with so many people on a weekly basis that have accepted the forgiveness of Christ, but then fail to step into His amazing proclamation of who they could be and the path and calling that Christ prepared for them. Instead of stepping completely into whom they were created to be, and helping take others to the top of their spiritual life, they choose a much lower elevation lifestyle; One that is akin to someone sitting at base camp on Mt. Everest, surrounded by all sorts of baggage and equipment but never climbing to the peak; Never helping any other person ascend to their highest. Instead, they sit amongst their baggage thinking that this is what life is all about. Close to the peak, and even submerged in the environment and culture of the climbers, yet remaining affixed to a lower elevation, living in the shadow of their greatest opportunity.

The higher you climb the less baggage you can take. Every climber starts out with gear and equipment, but their load always becomes lighter and lighter at each leg of the climb so that by the time he reaches the top, he has only the

> The higher you climb the less baggage you can take.

bare essentials with him. Unfortunately, too many followers of Christ never climb out of their baggage. They relate to Saul more than they realize; they are called to be kings yet live the life of a serf.

It was Jesus who said that if you want to be great in the Kingdom of God then you have to serve.[26] So it's obvious that we need to serve others. So what stops us? What keeps us from helping and serving others on a daily basis? It's definitely not a lack of opportunity. We fail to serve because we fail to take our eyes off of our own needs, issues, and insecurities long enough to see that others are in dire straits. The crazy thing is that if we really are walking with Christ, then He has already done everything to meet each of our needs and issues. If we fail to experience it then it is only because we find ourselves focusing on our baggage instead of on the declaration of freedom that Jesus bought for us. As you read the next chapter on what Christ accomplished for us, go ahead and pinpoint, and possibly even write down, specific issues in your life that you have been holding on to and are even using as an excuse as to why you haven't been reaching out to others. Because in all reality, Jesus has provided everything, in every area, for us to live a life completely free and unencumbered from the issues that daily plague us.

SHERPA CHECKLIST

1. Do you think you are insecure? If so, then in what areas?

2. How does knowing your specific role at work or home help in making you feel more secure in who you are?

3. What emotional baggage are you still holding on to? How is this baggage keeping you in a victim mindset rather than an overcomer mindset?

6

JESUS DID IT ALL

EASTER IS PRECEDED BY A week that we don't celebrate much...okay, ever. It is the week leading up to Easter that Jesus endured a torturous beating, an unfair trial, and of course the infamous death by crucifixion; which by itself, stands as a testimony to how thin the veneer of humanity truly is. During these torturous few days, Jesus walked out the prophecies that foretold the events of his death, and with each prophecy, and with each drop of blood from the body of Christ, we discover numerous areas where Jesus provided for us. Here, we find the answers to many of our struggles, and if we can wrap our arms and spirits around the profound provisions that Christ accomplished, then we can step into those benefits and experience the freedom and healing that we've always wanted and needed. Then once again, turn our attention and affection to those that have not yet found the saving grace of Christ.

THE GARDEN

The first place that Jesus bled for us was in the Garden of Gethsemane. The Bible tells us that as he prayed sweat like drops of blood fell to the ground.[27] Ironically, the first drops of blood that he shed were in a Garden, and a garden is where the battle first started. It was in the Garden where Adam and Eve lost the battle with the enemy. They allowed sin to enter into the world through their disobedience, where they knew and had heard God's will over the situation. I'm not sure God could have made it any more clear when he said, "Hey, ya'll can eat whatever you want in here. It's all-good for you. But see this tree right here? Don't eat from this one."[28]

They knew the Father's will, but they chose their own will over His and really messed things up for the rest of us. Ever since that moment, man has really been hopeless, but thankfully Jesus finds Himself in another garden battling with the exact same thing: His will. It was such a struggle for Him that his anguish turned his sweat into drops of blood; blood that was spilled for us.

My dream in life was to be an Architect. Every class I took in high school and technology school was geared towards propelling me into this field of work. An undercurrent to this was the idea that I knew I was called into the ministry. Unlike some people who wanted to be in the ministry, I did not. To me, it honestly seemed like a dead end job. In the field of Architecture I could emulate and look up to men like Frank Lloyd Wright and Frank Gehry. Growing up in church, the only examples I had of Pastors to look up to were old men. All of which seemed to be held to an unwritten code of ethics that included, but was not limited to, polyester suits, short hair (or the infamous comb-over), and the ability to tell the same boring story repeatedly without ever remembering the frequency to which it had been shared. But I knew deep down that God was calling me.

So like the good kid that I was, I pulled a Jonah and did my very best to run from God's voice and do exactly what I wanted to do. I graduated high school and enrolled in an architectural school in Detroit, where I immersed myself in my studies and was making a solid 4.0. Yet even with what seemed to be a natural place for me to be in life, I could not have been more miserable. No matter how many things went right, I was still eaten up with an insatiable desire, which was not my desire, but God's; until one Sunday, when it all came to a head. I was in my apartment in Detroit, and I knelt down at my multi-stacked stereo system to change the cassette tape out and I muttered to myself, "Life stinks." And as if God was right next to me, He said, "If you would have listened to me the first time you wouldn't be in the situation you're in now."

I stood up from that stereo with a new clear sense of who I was. The next morning I withdrew from architectural school and followed the path that God had laid out for me. Jesus shed blood in the garden in a battle of the wills. It is possible to know God's will for your life. He created you with a purpose and a plan. He doesn't keep it from us as a grand mystery; rather it's a battle of the wills, His versus ours. The great thing is that through the blood of Christ, which was shed in the garden, we have the ability and opportunity to know His will for our lives and to not live out a seemingly miserable existence always thinking there is more.

BRUISED FOR OUR INIQUITIES

In the book of Matthew, we read that Jesus was beat with a staff or rod, causing bruising all over his body.[29] Through modern day research we all know that a bruise is a broken blood vessel that bleeds internally close to the skin. Some of the most intense pain happens on the inside of us. In fact there have been times in my life where the heart-hurt was so painful, that if you could take it away by simply breaking my arm, I would have let you. Many times external pain is much more tolerable than the pain that happens in our hearts and emotions. It's the pain on the inside that you just can't seem to rub or caress.

The divorce, betrayal, or even the vicious words of a former friend, all hurt and wound us where no one can see. When I lost my father to bone cancer a few years ago it was a pain that didn't just go away overnight. People tried their very best to say the right things to offer comfort, but words just can't fill the void. I was not hurt, offended or even upset at some of the silly things people tend to say in times like that, because I understood that nobody really knows what to say, and anything that they could say would really just be powerless against that aching feeling on the inside.

> The intense, internal pain that all too often sets up inside our hearts is the very reason that Jesus shed His blood for us; it's the reason He sustained bruising.

The intense, internal pain that all too often sets up inside our hearts is the very reason that Jesus shed His blood for us; it's the reason He sustained bruising. Jesus knew, God knew, that heartache happens to us mortals. It's part of being, well, mortal. So in His amazing mercy He provided a way to fill the aching hole that is in so many hearts. He is the solution and the ointment to healing the internal pain. But it's a solution that we must align ourselves with, and accept.

FLOGGED FOR OUR HEALING

Of course, not all pain is internal and emotional. Let's be honest, there are some sicknesses out there that hurt pretty bad and we need the gift of healing. Isaiah 53 is a prophecy that says, *"By His stripes we are healed."* And then you flip over to Matthew 27 and see where Jesus was whipped causing blood to flow in rivulets down His back. Now, when we start talking about physical healing, people seem to always have stories. It's either the story of the divine miracle where their sister's aunt's first nephew's friend had their ears lowered or something. Then you try and track down the story and it turns into an urban legend like people waking up in a tub of ice with a note that tells them their kidneys have been cut out and to call 911.

Divine healing is real because I've seen it. I've experienced it in my own body and I've prayed for people and seen them healed. Through the stripes on His back our healing has been supplied, but I think the problem comes when we expect healing to come in a specific way at a specific time not allowing God to do it His way.

For a small amount of time in my ministry, I really got into the healing movement. I had seen a couple of people genuinely healed and that was just enough motivation for me to jump in with both feet, letting loose of all common sense. Now you might say that was faith, but if you knew me you'd know that it wasn't faith, it was naivety. With two healings under my proverbial belt, I went out into the marketplace to find my next victim. Walmart seemed like the perfect storm to find mangled people.

I walked in needing nothing except to find somebody in a wheel chair or on crutches, maybe sneezing, which would work just fine. As I walked into the musty air of the Suburban Shopping Mecca, my heart started beating a wee bit faster. Any normal person would recognize this as a sign of fear and would turn and run, but not me, I'm just not that smart. I prayed and asked God to show me somebody that needed healing and then I just turned and looked around. Imagine my delight when I saw a man standing behind the customer service counter on crutches! I couldn't see his legs because of the counter but that was not important. What was important, was that this was obviously a sign from the Lord that a healing hoe-down was about to begin!

I sauntered over to the counter with all the confidence of a calf at a new gate and the man smiled and said, "Can I help you?"

To which I replied, "What's wrong with your leg?" Fully hoping it was something manageable like a sprained ankle, or just an orthopedic boot.

"Oh, I just had a little accident a while ago."

"So did you sprain your ankle, break your foot? What happened?"

"It was just an accident a while ago. Is there something I can help you with?"

By this time, he was looking very uncomfortable and kept shifting his weight back and forth from one crutch to the next. I took that to be his cue that he wanted me to keep asking more and more personal questions that I had no business asking or knowing. I thought about pulling out the good ole' line from the book of Acts, "Silver and gold have I not, but what I have, I give unto thee!" BAM! And then jump over the counter and lay hands on the heathen, bringing healing and redemption to his soul. But instead, I opted for the more politically correct approach. I asked him, "If you'll show me what's wrong, I have something that can help."

I guess I poked and prodded enough at his privacy that he finally had reached his breaking point. My questions had probed and dug deep down into the past recesses of his mind, drudging up years of hurt, pain and agony, and undoing years of counseling. His face turned beet red and with great effort he swung the remaining nub of his leg up onto the counter and yelled, "I was 16 years old and was hit by an 18 wheeler! I haven't had a leg for over 15 years, what do you have that could possible help that?" I opened my mouth to speak but nothing came out. This is not how it was supposed to go. This was not the healing that I had envisioned in my mind, and this was altogether awkward. Without a word, I turned and walked out, leaving him standing there with his one nub leg on the counter and him glaring a hole in the back of my head.

Too often we pray for healing for ourselves or for someone else and we have it all figured out in our mind without ever considering that God might want to do it differently. We get so focused on the *how* that we forget all about the *who*. Then as we stand there, astonished that it

We get so focused on the *how* that we forget all about the *who*.

didn't go exactly like we planned, we begin doubting the powerful gift of healing that was provided for us in the blood of Christ.

I have learned over time that God does in fact heal; in fact, He heals in 3D. He heals divinely. There are some times, not all the time, but sometimes when he Heals people by working a divine miracle. I was standing next to a deaf man in Cuzco, Peru when the Lord miraculously opened his ears. No tricks, no mirrors, no doubt. I knew the man when he was deaf, and I talked with the man after the miracle and he could hear. It truly was a divine miracle.

Of course every healing is not exactly like that. He not only heals divinely, but he also heals through doctors. I thank God for technology and the knowledge that He has bestowed on man. It is a beautiful gift that can cure the sick and increase the length of our lives. To think that a man can reach inside another man's chest and fix his heart is truly a miracle of Godly proportions, and that doctor can only do that through the gifts and talents that God placed in him.

Finally, the Lord heals us through death. We don't like this one. Nobody wants to die, but the truth of the matter, is that we are all going to. There is no getting

We don't always like the way God chooses to bring healing into our lives, but His way is always the best way.

around it. The human mortality rate is steady at 100%, but we also know and believe that eternal life with Christ is pain-free and glorious. We don't always like the way God chooses to bring healing into our lives, but His way is always the best way. In Isaiah, He told us that His thoughts are by far higher, and loftier than ours and we need to trust in that and have faith that God always has our eternal best interest at heart.[30]

CROWN OF THORNS

Matthew 27 tells us that the next thing they did to His body was that they formed a crown for Him made out of thorns and then pushed it down, causing the long thorns to dig deep into the thin flesh on His head. The pain must have been excruciating, but it was pain with a purpose. Through that blood we find redemption for our thoughts and minds.

One of the largest battlefields in our spiritual walk is in our minds. It's there that we decide to follow Christ and it's in the same mind that after we decide to follow His ways, we doubt if we are saved. One minute we can think we are good and life is grand, and then in the next moment, fear and doubt can run rampant in our heads. Our minds have the propensity to betray us. If you have been in the church for any length of time you have probably read and even heard a sermon or two on 2 Corinthians 10:3-6, but don't dismiss it too quickly. Let's look at a couple of things first.

For though we walk in the flesh, we are not waging war according to the flesh. For the weapons of our warfare are not of the flesh but have divine power to destroy strongholds. We destroy arguments and every lofty opinion raised against the knowledge of God, and take every thought captive to obey Christ, being ready to punish every disobedience, when your obedience is complete.

So we have been given weapons to fight not in the flesh, but rather we have spiritual weapons to destroy strongholds. A stronghold is a good bible word that simply means 'a place in your life that has a strong hold over you.' It's that thing that you can't seem to shake, even though you've been walking with Jesus for 25 years. You still have that area, that thing that just will not seem to let go or leave you alone. That's a stronghold. But this verse tells us that we have been provided with

> It's that thing that you can't seem to shake, even though you've been walking with Jesus for 25 years.

weapons specifically to tear that junk down. But where is the stronghold? The next verse tells us what we are equipped to destroy. We have been fitted with the weapons to destroy arguments, doubt, and any thought that is contrary to the ways of Christ. Notice that all of those happen in the mind. It's in our mind that strongholds take up residence.

When I was a teenager I had developed a stronghold of lust. Maybe it was puberty gone wild, I don't know, but what I do know is my thoughts were constantly focused on lustful things. No matter what I tried, I couldn't stop my mind from going down that path. I mean seriously, how do you stop a thought from popping into your head? Every time I turned around, there was another girl, it seemed as if only girls had suddenly occupied the planet, it was terrifying! Then I read this verse in 2 Corinthians and I found hope. I couldn't stop the thoughts from coming but I at least had the power to take them as prisoners since they were dark thoughts trespassing in a redeemed mind. I decided that every time a lustful thought would pop into my head I would say out loud, "That is not a godly thought. I take that thought captive to the obedience of Christ." Needless to say, I got a lot of strange looks, but it seemed to work almost instantly. The thoughts would temporarily stop.

Over the next several months the thoughts became more and more spaced out and then the struggle switched from deterring the thoughts to choosing the right thoughts. Of course I didn't always choose the right thoughts, but the more I did, the easier it became. The more I focused on stopping the thoughts the more hopeless and despondent I became, but I realized that stopping the thoughts is ridiculous, but capturing them is scriptural.

PIERCED HANDS

I hate a limp handshake. If you're a man, or a boy, and I stick my hand out to shake yours, please do not hand me a limp mackerel. Grab my hand and give it a firm squeeze. Don't try to crush it, just squeeze it. I'm sure you're strong and manly because you have taken Uncle Rico's work out videos so seriously and you have used your hand exerciser for days on end to improve your grip, but crushing the bones in my hand is not necessary. Somewhere in between the dead fish and the bone crusher is a normal handshake. Normal is good. A handshake is how most adults begin a relationship. We extend a hand of welcome in one manner or another.

Often times in the bible, hands are symbolic of relationships. Many times in the Bible we read where someone stretched out their hand to bless someone, and even in that blessing a relationship is understood to exist. You wouldn't bless someone you didn't know or care about, and the same holds true here. They pierced the hands of Jesus with nails as they secured him to the cross. That blood from his hands offers redemption for our broken relationships.

One thing that always needs to be worked on after you come to Christ is relationships. As a whole, we are not very good at relationships. It's a tough area that offers a lot of challenges. From friendships gone awry, to marriages falling apart; it seems that getting along with others is still a tall order to fill. To answer Rodney King's infamous quote: No, we can't all get along. Most of the counseling I do for others ends up being about them getting along with someone else, and most of the time it comes down to them needing to forgive the other person.

I sat down yesterday and talked with a guy named Derrick. One of his main struggles was that he was holding grudges against anybody and everybody in his life that had wronged him or disappointed him in one way or another. I asked him if he had forgiven them and he said, "Yeah,

I've forgiven them but I just can't seem to let it go. Everybody tells me to just let it go but I can't seem to do it. It's not that easy." Derrick was trying to separate forgiveness and letting things go. However, they are one and the same. Since Derrick was unable to let these things go it caused him to begin living a life that was completely focused on himself. He was unable to lead anybody up any mountain, and was unable to see anything except his own problems and issues that others apparently had caused in his life. He loved God and was doing his best to follow Christ, but his Christian walk now resembled a one legged man attempting to rock the Cupid Shuffle. It wasn't pretty.

When our relationships are out of whack, more times than not, it's because we have not employed the power of forgiveness. We find ourselves in the same boat as Derrick. We love Jesus, and we say we have forgiven others, but we can't seem to just let it go. Then we begin a slow, downward spiral that causes us to only think about our own issues and ourselves. Not having our relationships redeemed and in order affects every area of our lives. Everything is based on relationships. Think about it, most of us have the jobs we have because we knew the right person. We hear about a sale because we knew somebody. We go to the church we go to because we knew someone who attended there; the list goes on and on. In fact, you can't even get into Heaven unless you know the right person! Relationships are so powerful that Jesus taught us that if your relationships were not in order it would affect how you worship and serve in the Kingdom of God.[31] We have to forgive, and forgiving truly is letting go of it, and that's a tall order. Derrick knew he had to let go of the grudges and issues but he didn't know how. He needed an action step not another well-meaning grandma muttering, "Just let go." Derrick needed to learn *how* to let go.

When a relationship goes awry and you find yourself holding on to unforgiveness, and perhaps even bitterness, the best way to forgive

There is a profound link between the confession of our mouths and the health of our spiritual man.

is to tell yourself that you forgive them. When a nasty or negative thought about Sister Sally comes to mind, say out loud, "I choose not to think about that because I forgive Sister Sally." Now at first this will seem weird and awkward, but there is a profound link between the confession of our mouths and the health of our spiritual man. The first day you employ this tactic you might have 600 thoughts about Sister Sally, and 600 times you need to say out loud, "No, I forgive Sister Sally." The second day it might only be 567 and then the third day 432, and so on and so on until all of a sudden you realize that Sister Sally no longer consumes your thoughts. You are no longer holding on to that grudge, because you have genuinely forgiven her. It doesn't mean you forget. Forgive and forget is the stupidest wives tale in the history of the world. You're not a moron, you can remember the pain and issues that Sister Sally caused, but forgiveness is a choice that once we employ it and apply it to our lives, we find ourselves able to focus not on her and the issues, but on other things in life.

While we are on the subject of messed up relationships, let me say that there is a profound difference between forgiving someone and trusting someone.

There is a profound difference between forgiving someone and trusting someone.

Forgiveness is a must. It's an unequivocal fact found numerous places in the bible. The bible goes so far as to say that the only way to have our own sins forgiven is to model it by forgiving others. But trust is a totally different story. Forgiveness is a gift, but trust is earned. You go to work and you earn a paycheck; you earn your wage. Trust is the wage that is paid over time in a healthy relationship. So even if someone continually messes up your world and is the worst person on the planet, yes, you really can forgive them. But that does not mean that you are biblically bound to trust them. They have to earn that.

PIERCED FEET

You know the old saying, "Don't shoot yourself in the foot." I've heard it a lot but it didn't stop me. To make matters even more interesting, it was during a youth Halloween outreach event. I was the Youth Pastor and I had this great idea to do a thing called, "The House of Death." It was similar to a haunted house but we would take people through and show them different death scenes and then lead them into Heaven and Hell to show them that they had a choice. Basically, we did our best to scare the Hell out of them. It was great fun. One of the scenes involved a sawed off pistol grip 12 gauge shotgun. It was loaded with blanks, so really, what could go wrong? At the end of the first evening's show the actor brought me the gun because I was the responsible adult on duty, and being the responsible adult on duty, I took the gun and placed the barrel on my foot and then leaned on it like a cane, while chatting with some people.

I didn't hear the gun go off as much as I felt it. I felt it go off, along with my big toe. The good news was that my boot caught my dismembered toe so that those talented doctors could put it back on; which was a real bonus since I still needed them to count to twenty. Three surgeries, one skin graft,

> I didn't hear the gun go off as much as I felt it.

gallons of antibiotics, and six months of physical therapy later, walking became possible again. Walking is something that we definitely take for granted until the power to walk is stripped from us and we realize that everywhere we go requires walking. When we can't walk life becomes more difficult to say the least.

Jesus bled from the nail in his feet to redeem our walk through life. Once we step into a life with Him our walk should be a walk of confidence and authority. I'm continually amazed at how many followers of Christ walk through life playing the role of the victim. It seems like every situation they approach, they approach with a victim mindset, when Christ has provided for us the ability to walk in

Once we step into a life with Him our walk should be a walk of confidence and authority.

authority. Jesus told His disciples in Luke 10:19, *"I have given you authority over all the power of the enemy and you can walk among snakes and scorpions and crush them."*[32] Obviously, the walking motif coincides with His feet being pierced, but it also reflects back to the Garden of Eden where God told Satan that his head would be crushed under the heel of man. That takes us into the New Testament world where Paul wrote, *"The God of peace will soon crush Satan under your feet."*[33] No matter how you slice it, Jesus provided authority for us and we should be walking in it.

The enemy is a strong, influential beast that has power. We minimize his fear instilling form thanks to the media and graphic artists that like to portrait him as a skinny dude in full spandex with little horns and a cute tail. However, there is nothing further from the truth. Just because you might think of him that way doesn't change who he is. And while Satan has power, we have authority.

Understanding the difference between authority and power is crucial. If you're a football fan then you understand that you can have a lineman that is 6' 5" weighing in at 380 pounds. He can pulverize anything that gets in front of him; he is the definition of power. But then you have this guy that is 5' 10" weighing in at 136 pounds wearing a black and white striped shirt and even though he has

Understanding the difference between authority and power is crucial.

obviously less power than the linebacker, he has the authority to stop him in his tracks. In fact, he even has the authority to go nose to nose with the behemoth player and kick him out of the game. Authority always supercedes power.

It's this kind of authority that Christ provided for us that overrides the attacks of the enemy in our lives, and in our homes, if we will but walk in it.

THE 5 ½ MILE HIGH CLUB | 71

PIERCED SIDE

The final place that Jesus bled for us was His side.[34] A lot of times we think of God as angry and distant, but the whole point of Christ coming was to bridge the gap. The real heart of the matter was to restore what was broken. He came and became like us so that He could redeem us. He isn't mad, or angry at our shortcomings. Can I tell you that His heart breaks for us? His heart was broken and is broken even today for the things that He sees us going through. He hears our prayers, and He hears our cries of anguish and pain. He knows that this walk of life has moments that are not comfortable. In fact, there are many times and moments where it's down right painful and we just don't understand. We have questions on why marriage has to be so hard, why kids make such stupid choices, why money and life are just too hard, yet through all that Jesus' heart breaks. He is the only one that can truly say, "I understand."

If we believe and follow that line of reasoning then the very next question that is on our lips is, "Then why doesn't He fix it or change it?" There are so many difficult situations where we wish He would just swoop down and fix it, change it, transform it...but He doesn't. I can't explain all of it but I do know this – this is not Heaven. When Heaven comes it will be perfect and glorious, but right now we are here, in this fallen world dealing with fallen things. But in the midst of the fallen world we still have hope. Hope for heaven and hope for tomorrow. It is through his pierced and broken heart that He comes alongside us and puts His arm around us and says, "I love you. I'm here for you."

There is a desperate need in the Kingdom of God for the followers of Christ to recognize the seven ways that Christ bled, and then align themselves with the complete and full redemption that has been provided. When we don't do this we live our entire lives focused on ourselves and our own issues and problems while ignoring the plight,

When we don't do this we live our entire lives focused on ourselves and our own issues and problems while ignoring the plight, pain, and peril of the lost that is all around us. pain, and peril of the lost that is all around us. When Jesus told us to pray for laborers for the harvest, in essence He's saying we need more people that can be focused on something else besides themselves, because everything that they could ever want or need has already been provided for them in the complete atonement of Christ. Now, it's a matter of recognizing that, aligning ourselves with it, and then turning our attention once again to getting more people up the mountain so that they too can experience and have their pinnacle moment with Jesus Christ.

SHERPA CHECKLIST

1. Of all the things that that Christ provided for us, which are you needing to walk in the most?

2. Who do you still need to forgive?

3. Even though we step into the forgiveness of Christ, how often do you not offer that forgiveness to others?

4. What specific area of your life would be better if you walked in the authority that Christ has already provided and granted?

7

DEATH IS BECOMING

DEATH IS ONE THING THAT is guaranteed to happen to all of us, and it's the one thing that the majority of people have trepidations about. Even though we've been taught and have read in the Bible that death is not the end, there is more living to be done after this thing called death. Even though we know all that, it doesn't stop us from fearing the unseen and the inevitable. That's one reason most people hate funerals. Talk of death, seeing death, and being reminded of our own mortality is unnerving to many. But death comes to everyone, and funerals, like it or not, are common.

I, personally, have done more funerals than I can count. I've done joyful ones, sad ones, tragic ones and crazy ones. The first funeral that I ever officiated over was during my time as a youth pastor. I was 23 years old and one of the girls in my youth group had a baby who tragically died after living a mere two weeks. Needless to say, when I stood up to deliver the message, I was shaking in my pants. I honestly can't remember another time where I have been that nervous. But I painfully got through it and then all that was left to be done was the graveside service. I had never done a graveside ceremony either, but I had seen it done, so how hard could it really be? Read a scripture, say a prayer, give condolences to the family, and then head to the house.

The scripture came off without a hitch and the prayer was flawless, I was impressed with myself to say the least. All that was left was to walk down the front row and shake hands with the family members sharing my deepest sympathies with them as I worked my way to my car. I looked down the front row of family, which was parallel to the casket, and realized that there was not a lot of room between their feet and the gaping hole in the ground. Whoever had set up the chairs for the day's event obviously wanted the family as close to their deceased as possible. At this point, my brain processed something that was along the lines of, "Hey buddy, not a lot of room there to walk, you might just want to wave, dismiss the crowd and then give condolences." But we have already established that I'm a guy, and therefore I am not the sharpest tool in the shed, and long term processing is not really in my DNA. So instead of taking that advice, I convinced myself that my lithe like frame could easily slink through the slim opening and successfully perform all of my pastoral duties.

Allow me to pause here, and uncomfortably share with you that the mother of the deceased was extremely well endowed, and had decided that a funeral was the proper time and place to display all that the Lord had endowed her with. My first step into the sliver of space between the casket and the family brought me to grandpa. I shook his hand and muttered something about 'sorry for your loss,' while the whole time my foot was in the forefront of my mind, because in just one step I realized that there was only enough room for my shoe. One side of my shoe was up against grandpa's chair leg and the other side was up against the little frame that was blocking roaming people from falling into the pit of despair that loomed like an open mouth beneath the casket.

The next hand was grandma, and then some dude I didn't know. I was wiggling and writhing my way down the row when I had almost gotten to the mom. I took a tentative baby step to shorten the distance to her, and when I did, my foot landed on top of the brace that was supporting the casket. I didn't see it because the grounds keepers were also fashion conscious and decided to cover the brace in lovely indoor-outdoor carpet, which made it as slippery as a greased hog on a rainy spring afternoon. My foot landed and immediately slipped off the brace, which caused me to fall, but obviously I didn't want to fall into the pit of despair, so I twisted my 120 pound frame the other direction and stepped on a chair leg which caused both feet to go flying up into the air, propelling me completely horizontally onto the laps of the family, laying face up. I thought I had possibly blacked out since my eyes were open, but all I could see was black. But then, to my chagrin, I realized that my face was wedged under the awning of the mother's large endowment. The mom pressed her endowment back unveiling my face and said, "You always make me laugh." I'm glad, because laughter is always better than a sexual assault charge.

DEATH ZONE

Death is not a comfortable topic, or a comfortable place. On Mt. Everest, there is a place known as the Death Zone. In order to reach the summit, a climber must acclimate to the rigorous elevation through a series of climbs and descents, but you can't acclimatize to the death zone. Once you are above 24,000 feet your body can no longer adjust to the lack of oxygen and the lack of pressure. If a climber were taken from sea level immediately to the summit of Mt. Everest without acclimating first, they would black out within minutes. But with acclimatization, a climber can last several days in the Death Zone. The Death Zone is not a fun walk in the park, but in order to reach the summit and in order to help others reach the summit, we have to get used to the death.

It almost seems counter productive to talk about death when really we're supposed to be all about life, but Jesus seemed to see it the other way around. He taught that you couldn't even have real abundant life until you first have death.[35] Death precedes life, not vise versa. Now

He taught that you couldn't even have real abundant life until you first have death.

before you think Jesus was offering a little red Kool-Aid, Jim Jones style religion, let me say that I'm convinced He was not. What He is opening our eyes to is the concept that if we will put to death all of our own sins, lusts, and fleshly desires, then we will be in a position to live a full and abundant life.

Once of my favorite verses in the Bible is John 10:10 where Jesus said, *"I have come that you may have life, and life more abundantly."* That verse rocks my world! But, what I have realized over the years is that I don't always experience that kind of over the top abundant living. I've tried to blame it on Jesus and His lack of delivering the goods, but every time, when I look closely at what's going on, I realize that I am the one stopping the flow of abundant life. It's that old me

When I keep the zombie in the grave and make sure that the death of my old ways is a priority, then the life of Christ blossoms.

trying to come back to life in some sort of sick, zombie like way, trying to fight for my own selfish ways and desires to be met. When I keep the zombie in the grave and make sure that the death of my old ways is a priority, then the life of Christ blossoms and I realize that there truly is life and more abundant life at that, to be experienced.

We have to experience a Death Zone if we are going to help others meet Christ because it's not always fun and enjoyable; sometimes it's flat out hard work. But when our efforts are not divided between our own selfish ways and God's ways, then we are more focused and acclimated for the climb. We can embrace the death that needs to occur in each of us so that we can in turn embrace the life that Christ has for us as we escort others to the summit.

Jesus dealt with dead people several times in the bible. He resurrected a young girl who had been dead for a few minutes, a boy who had been dead at least a whole day, and then he resurrected Lazarus who had been dead for four days.[36] Which of those three people were deader? Hopefully you didn't choose the first one because last time I checked, dead is still dead. There are not degrees to dead, you're either living or you're not, not a lot of in between room. But when it comes to the death and burial of our sin, we unfortunately categorize it based on its severity, regularity, and uniqueness.

LAZARUS EFFECT

Lazarus is a great example of how it is not until after death that you become more effective in peoples lives. Lazarus was one of Jesus' good friends. The Bible tells us that his family had a special place in his heart and they often visited each other. So Lazarus had the teaching of Jesus in him. He was a follower of Christ and believed in who He was and what He was doing; yet Lazarus was not a huge influencer before his death. Here was a man that had the teaching and had even accepted the beauty of Christ into his life and very literally into his home, yet failed to make a viable impact in his town.

One day, while Jesus was away preaching, he received a message that Lazarus was sick. We read that since Jesus loved him so much, he waited two more days to make sure that Lazarus was good and dead.[37] He could have left right then and possibly made it back to heal Lazarus before he died, but his love for Lazarus was so great, and he was so special to Jesus that He waited. He waited because he knew that more people could be touched, changed and impacted through the life of Lazarus if he would experience death first.

The actual resurrection of Lazarus is a powerful and well-known bible story. Part of the story was the first bible verse I ever memorized, mostly because it is also the shortest. "Jesus wept." You just have to love short and easy memory verses. The resurrection of Lazarus is so well known that often times our attention gets wrapped up in the event and fails to realize the impact of the aftermath.

Before Lazarus had died, the Gospel had been taught. It was present in his life and in his family, but no social change had happened through him. All too often, this is the story of the majority of Christians. We find ourselves having the teachings of Christ resonating in our lives and homes, yet it never flows through us to impact our world. Our neighborhoods are the same, our places of work are the same, and our schools are the same. Lazarus was dead for four days before Christ resurrected him. This event impacted the life of Lazarus so much that he became a catalyst for change in his community. He

> It's not until we experience death, that we can experience life.

was dead and resurrected in John 11, and then in the very next chapter, we see a totally changed Lazarus. Up until this point, the Jews were plotting to kill only Jesus, but now they are plotting to kill Jesus and Lazarus as well. So many people were turning to Christ because of the impact that Lazarus was having on them that the Jews could no longer ignore him. Lazarus had become a revolutionary for the cause.

When Jesus comes back to town He goes over Lazarus' house to eat and, like all good friends, Lazarus throws a party for him, and the house was packed. People came from out of town, not only to see Jesus, but the Bible says they came to see Lazarus as well. All these out of town people were the same people, who the very next day, shouted, cheered, and threw down their cloaks for Jesus to make his triumphal entry into town on a colt. Lazarus became an integral part of making Jesus famous. Not because of what he did, because let's be honest, Lazarus didn't have much to say about being resurrected, all he did was lay there. But the power

> But the power changing moment didn't come in the form of action as much as it came in the form of reaction.

changing moment didn't come in the form of action as much as it came in the form of reaction. His reaction to what Jesus did for him is the key. In that moment he realized that he couldn't keep living the way he was living, something had to change.

It's the same with us. We are totally powerless in having our sins forgiven. The grace of God that makes it all possible is a completely free gift with no strings attached. Once we step into that grace and experience it, then the reaction to it will either be extremely powerful and world changing, or mundane and sedentary. I vote for world changing. Churches have enough sedentary members. Your world, not the entire globe, but your world; those people and places that your life revolves around, those people you see and talk to everyday, need you. They need you to be dead to your self-centered outlook on life and they genuinely need you to serve and guide them to that pinnacle moment in Christ. How we get to do that is the fun part.

SHERPA CHECKLIST

1. What "zombie-moments" have you experienced lately in your own life?

2. What areas of your life need to be put to death?

3. What "living-areas" are consistently keeping you from serving others?

8

MESSY CHURCH IS GODLY CHURCH

RULE-FEST

CHURCH HAS RULES. EVERYBODY KNOWS it; they just don't know which rules each church holds up as the highest commodity. I am of course not talking about biblical standards, but rather social standards that fit the culture of where you are. For example, you would never eat a hotdog at a Vegan festival, nor would you wear a hat into a church building. If that were to happen then God would strike you dead immediately, after all it's in the Bible! Um, no. No it's not. As well as a plethora of other things that we hold up as sacred rules that are required for proper church to take place, even though you can't find them anywhere in the Bible. I understand that each church has their distinctive rules that make it what it is, but some of the things that we call church distinctives are actually things that deter people from God and the church, rather than draw them in.

But some of the things that we call church distinctives are actually things that deter people from God and the church, rather than draw them in.

We have dress codes, inside jokes, and even our own language. Basically, most churches are structured and run like a church for only church people. If you do not wear the right clothes or use the correct holy verbiage to describe how your week went, then you are obviously out of place.

One of the leaders in our church took their kids to a Vacation Bible school at another church in our town. She did that mainly because we don't offer one. I have had different people in our church ask for one or hint at starting one, to which I always reply, "Why don't you take your kids to such and such church down the road, they have a great VBS." We try not to do anything that another church in our town is already doing well, but of course that's just my philosophy and doesn't have a whole lot to do with my story or my point. So, one of the leaders took her kids to such and such church for their VBS program. On the final day they closed with a typical service inviting all the parents to come and see their kids graduate from the grueling 3 day VBS.

Our leader thought nothing of showing up to the afternoon service/graduation wearing jeans and a shirt. Nothing fancy, but nothing slouchy either. At the close of the service an elderly lady walked up to my friend and said, "I'm glad you're here, but when you come back next time, I expect you to be wearing something more appropriate for the house of the Lord." To which my friend replied, "Oh you don't have to worry about that, I won't be back. Ever."

Being in church my entire life, people never cease to amaze me. Never. I have watched time and time again, people push their own traditions and rules on hungry, seeking people instead of laying aside all of the traditions of man and simply escorting the weary climber to the top of the mountain to meet Jesus. We have to get to a point where it's okay to have lost people in the church. It will do no good if you go out into the highways and hedges to bring them in, if the party you are bringing them to, has so many regulations that they can't even get in once they arrive.

Many churches will put herculean effort into various outreach events to meet new people who seem to be seeking answers to life. Yet these people never seem to stick, and the churches never seem to grow. Could it be that once these people arrive they feel put out, marginalized and basically unwelcome? Could it be that we

> We strive so hard to make our buildings and gatherings sanctified and holy that we have actually become quite pompous in our beliefs.

have become so church focused that we have forgotten to be people focused? We strive so hard to make our buildings and gatherings sanctified and holy that we have actually become quite pompous in our beliefs.

DOOR STOPS

In the second chapter of Mark we read a story about a paralyzed guy who had been brought to Jesus. Jesus was in a house teaching and the throngs of people were jam packed in there and even spilled out the door, making it impossible for the friends to get their paralyzed buddy in to see Jesus. So as the story goes, they climbed up on the roof and dug a hole, then lowered their friend right down into the middle of the crowd in front of Jesus. Jesus forgives him of his sins and then heals him. Now you would think that the crowd would go crazy with joy, but instead they become disgruntled and start to complain.

> The paralytic with the greatest problem couldn't even get in to the house to see the Great Physician because the door was blocked by church folk who were only there to find fault.

They complained because there was some forgiveness being thrown around in there and that was just not the way it had always been done before. Jesus forgiving the man of his sins rocked their world. That was not normal, it was also not normal to allow a sinner like that to be in their midst. The paralytic with the greatest problem couldn't even get in to the house to see the Great Physician because the door was blocked by church folk who were only there to find fault.

I know that's extreme, and you immediately think that your church is not that harsh. I hope it's not, but one way or the other, we have to begin to realize that doing church the way we have always done it is not going to create the right atmosphere and culture for lost people to come and experience the presence of God. We can, and should, serve them in the community and in our places of work, but they also need a place to come; a safe place to come and connect with God and then download good things from him.

> They also need a place to come; a safe place to come and connect with God and then download good things from him.

As a pastor, one of the things I have dealt with more than just about anything else is people who have been hurt by their church. They love God, but the Church chewed them up and spit them out for one reason or another. Many of those people have wandered into the doors of our church looking like an abused child at a family reunion: full of excuses and as skittish as an Enron Executive on April 15th. It takes time for them to acclimate and enjoy being in the house of God again. Every time I discover a person or couple that has been wounded by the Church, I go and apologize on behalf of the church and let them know that they can come and just do nothing for as long as they need to, so they can find the healing that they need.

We need, in our churches, an atmosphere where it is okay to not be okay; you just can't stay there. In other words, you can come just as you are; you can come with your junk, sin, and nasty issues. WARNING: That does mean that if those honest and real people are in your lobby and on your front porch, you will see things and hear things that might just cause you to blush. What happens if you hear somebody drop some serious curse words? I know some good old fashion church ladies that would gasp and then hit their knees in prayer begging God not to strike the building with fire and brimstone because they just got the church paid off.

I think God smiles. Now before you throw this book down as complete heresy, let me ask you a question. What temple, or church does the Holy Spirit live in? If you were in the Old Testament that would be an easy answer, the Tabernacle of course, but now that we are living in the New Testament the answer is different. It's no longer a building, but according to Jesus, now we are the temple of God. Not a church, cathedral, monastery, chapel, mosque, or basilica....nope, us; flesh and blood bodies. So if a person who is not claiming to follow Jesus, but is seeking Him, comes into our church and cusses, why would it upset God anymore than when the seeking person cusses at work? At least while she is at church she is seeking and is obviously one step closer to discovering her Savior.

ROTISSERIE

Unfortunately, we have set up our churches in the United States as holy places rather than realizing that Jesus specifically told us that they are not holy places, but rather we are holy vessels. As holy vessels we need to stop deterring people from discovering who their Savior is and accept them the way they are, and then serve them and lead them to that fantastic moment of meeting Jesus. Then, and only then, do we guide them to becoming a more beautiful reflection of their creator.

We want and expect instant transformation but that is not how God works. God is a rotisserie Deity in microwave culture. We even look at various miracles in the Bible, and since they are in one verse we just read into them the instantaneous part. In Exodus, Moses stands in between Pharaoh's army and the Red Sea. He raises his staff, and bam! The waters parted. At least that's how it was on the flannel graph in Sunday school. But that's not how the Bible says it happened. It says that Moses raised his staff and then *"all that night God drove back the waters."*[38] All that night is not instantaneous. All that night means hours upon hours. Was it a miracle? Absolutely, beyond a shadow of a doubt, it was. Could God have done it in an instant? Absolutely, beyond a shadow of a doubt, He could have. But He chose to do it through a process. It's this same process that He works in every single one of us.

When we first started SouthPoint a lady named Tracy came. She had received one of the fliers that we sent out announcing our new church and she held on to it. When that Sunday approached she got up and began getting ready.

Her boyfriend rolled over and said, "What are you doing?"

She said, "I'm going to church." To which he replied, "You can't go to church you don't believe in God!"

She didn't believe in God, but she was seeking. She felt an inside tug that said there is more to this life, and that someone, something she couldn't explain, loved her. She came to church as an atheist and left church that day as an atheist, but on the way out she stopped to talk to me. She said, "This is my first time here."

I glibly said back, "It's mine too; this is actually our first Sunday."

"I don't mean it like that," she said. "What I mean is, this is my first time to ever be in church. I've never attended a church service before, but if this is what God is all about you can count me in." and she turned and walked out. She walked in and out every Sunday for about six months. Never committing her life to Christ and never really changing on the outside, but she came every Sunday, accepted just like she was. No expectations just come as you are and be accepted. It took six months, but finally I got to watch as Tracy raised her hand at the close of service and accepted Jesus Christ as her personal Savior. She jumped on a volunteer team and served at the church for a couple of years until she finally decided to move back home to Boston where she became a leading team member at a brand new church launch there. She went from Atheist to church leader in less than five years.

How would her story be different if she was expected to change before she was changed? If there was no real lasting change in her soul space, yet she began acting like all the other church-goers that she saw, what would have happened then? I believe that is what we define as a hypocrite. Of course, Tracy is from Boston, so it is also true that if she would have been expected to change before there was change she would have either left with a bad taste in her mouth, or jabbed a pair of scissors in my eye. One way or the other, dynamic change takes time, and as the church we have to be patient with God's miraculous flow.

SHERPA CHECKLIST

1. What distinctives are you molding your life around?

2. What traditions in your life have you elevated above scripture?

3. What personal distincitves could be pushing people away instead of drawing them close?

4. Are you ever impatient with the spiritual process in your life? Are you less or more patient in that process in others?

5. Do you expect people to externally change before they are inwardly changed?

9
CHANGE OF PERSPECTIVE

I WAS DRIVING DOWN THE road the other day and I looked over and noticed a church that I had been driving by for several years had closed down. No sign for relocation or anything; just closed. No more church. The annoying thing to me was that it wasn't in the papers, and it didn't make the news. One day it was a church, and the next day an empty building. I thoroughly doubt that the entire congregation died on the exact same day, and I doubly doubt that the rapture took place and Jesus only came back for them.

The empty building got me thinking. The reason the church closing didn't make the news is probably because when the church was open for business it wasn't making the news. It wasn't impacting the community that it was in, in a newsworthy way. I decided at that moment that I wanted our church to be so involved in the community and the city, that if for some strange reason our church imploded and just disappeared, that the community would rise up and say, "Where's *that* church? Where are the ones that helped us, loved us, and gave us hope?"

DANGER OF SAFE CHURCH

Unfortunately, churches have become places where people retreat to find safety. It's almost as if each church is the Alamo. Run in, barricade the doors and hope the enemy never gets in. That plan might have been valiant in the 1800's, but let's be honest, they lost. Hiding inside the walls of the church will only cause the church to wither and die. I have yet to see a church that is completely inwardly focused, grow and be a healthy vibrant group of believers. In those situations what happens time and time again, is at some point somebody turns on somebody else and begins devouring them, and this begins the painful process of a church split; or at the very least an infestation of bitterness and gossip. Of course if you grew up like I did, then you're inwardly focused church home will erupt into an all out brawl in the center aisle of the church.

I was only about nine and as the Sunday night service was coming to a close, the pastor uttered the most horrific words known to any young boy. He said, "Immediately following service tonight we will have a short business meeting." The thought of having any daylight left to play when I got home, quickly evaporated as I settled in for another long boring church business meeting. What made it worse was that the business meeting was to appoint a committee to redecorate the parsonage that the pastor was living in. Even at the green age of nine I had sat in enough of these meetings to know that none of them were ever short, and none of them were ever interesting. Well, never interesting, until this one.

The idea of voting in a decorating committee was squashed by the pastor as he just appointed some people, and then somebody in the crowd yelled out that he was a liar and a cheat. This was obviously not following Robert's Rules of Order, and it seemed to get the congregation in a lather, which caused everyone to stand and start yelling. Luckily for me, my seat was right behind the lead instigator in this impromptu rebellion, so I got to see everything up close and personal. The Pastor's son who was twenty something in age and was the acting youth pastor, decided that he didn't like anybody calling his dad a liar and a cheat, so he decided to hurl curse words at the man from the other side of the sanctuary and then charge after him with fists clinched.

When the illustrious youth pastor got up to the man that was standing about 3 feet from me, he didn't pause or hesitate, but swung for all he was worth, and connected with a solid right hook to the jaw. I'm speculating at this point, but I believe he was hoping that his one punch would succinctly knock the church-attending heathen completely out or at least to his senses. However, it did neither. Instead, it seemed to unleash the bar room brawler that had been encased in the veneer of Christianity for a way too long. The lead instigator began to release a world of hurt on the young youth pastor like he had never seen or expected. It took several men to peel the large, burly man off of the pastor's son. Before there was MMA, there were church business meetings, and obviously the most interesting business meetings are the ones involving interior decorating.

However, when a church does what it was created to do, which is to bring hope, faith, and love to a broken and hurt community, then the mission of the church moves beyond its own pettiness and into a pursuit of the lost.

When a church is only looking inward, it will eventually turn on itself and begin fighting amongst itself over things that have absolutely no value or eternal weight. However, when a church does what it was created to do, which is to bring hope, faith, and love to a broken and hurt community, then the mission of the church moves beyond its own pettiness and into a pursuit of the lost.

For several years after college, I went on a study tangent of revivals. I read any and every book I could find on revivals in any and every country. I got excited reading about those historical events, because in those stories I saw genuine people who loved God, being amazingly touched in a powerful way. To read about crazy miracles and throngs of people coming to hear the message of Christ was exhilarating! Smith Wigglesworth, William J. Seymour, Aimee Semple McPherson, and Kathryn Kuhlman, just to name a few. The Chronicles of their lives was, and still is, mesmerizing to me. What they did ignited spiritual revivals around the globe, but the lasting fruit of what happened *then* appears to be lacking *now*.

When you look at the great historical moves of God through the scope of time, it almost seems as if these were just moments and not movements. They would flash up and gain a little ground, but then fizzle into nothingness, with nothing left to show that God had even been there. But what we read in the book of Acts is the polar opposite of that. In fact, the church of today is still riding the wave and momentum of that early church that had no money, no political backing and no social influence, yet they changed the spiritual climate of our world.

In fact, the church of today is still riding the wave and momentum of that early church that had no money, no political backing and no social influence, yet they changed the spiritual climate of our world.

INSIDE OUTSIDE IN

The most glaring difference between the early church in the book of Acts and the modern day moves of God is perspective. The view and perspective of most modern day revivals is about others coming into a gathering place where they can hear the word and experience the presence of God. Everything is central focused, meaning that you have to get in the building to feel God's life changing presence. You beg and cajole people to come into the House of the Lord to be touched and changed, and that's not a *bad* thing, it just can't be the *only* thing.

The early church in the book of Acts had their gathering places that we call church, where God showed up and did some amazing things. But the most astounding things that God did during those formidable days were not *in* the church but *outside* the church. It was at people's places of work, in their homes, and in their places of social interactions. Basically, they had the perspective that Jesus is awesome and we need to take this Good News to them, wherever they are.

The way they took the Good News to people should be a life lesson to all of us, and I believe it is the only way to see a self-sustaining move of God that lasts not a month or a year but a life time: they served. They went out of their candy coated safety shell into the culture of their day and found that people had needs, and then they would meet those needs. Not by yelling, screaming and trying to shove their version of Jesus down their throats, but rather humbly serving and making a difference in people's lives. I think we have all seen the ineffectiveness of the loud and condemning street preachers. They seem to offer no grace, no love, and no practical help.

I went with a team of ministers one year to Mardi Gras to do some street evangelism. Our method was not to preach at people, but rather to walk around, engage people in a one on one conversation, listen to them and then share how Jesus was the solution to their every need. It was amazing and we had numerous "God moment" conversations. I sat down next to a lady and her husband on the curb of Canal Street and began talking about nothing in particular, yet God was present. The conversation quickly turned to how she was hurting and seemed lost, because her grandmother had just passed away and she had raised her, and now she had no one to turn to. She felt completely alone and lost. She asked me, "Who do I go to now for help?" I was privileged to get to introduce her to her Savior that night.

I got up from that conversation feeling pretty good and decided to see who else I could find to talk with about this Good News. I headed down Bourbon Street and there was a group of about 8-10 street preachers set up in a formidable circle in the middle of the street, with a large wooden cross in the middle of the circle. Around the whole group were barricades that the police had set up to keep them safe and separated from the partiers. At first I thought the barricades were a bit overkill, until I got close enough to hear what the street preachers were yelling into their bullhorns; it was not nice. They were declaring that God hates this, and hates that, and that everyone was going to burn in Hell. I was pretty sure I was not going to burn in Hell so I decided that I needed to correct them.

I weaved my way through the crowd of partiers and the closer I got to the barricade the more hostile the atmosphere became. The area surrounding this band of preachers was tense, antagonistic, and dangerous. Partiers were yelling and throwing things at the preachers, and the preachers would hurl insults and condemning thoughts back, it was not a fun place. I leaned over the barricade and told the closest preacher and said, "Hey man! We're on the same team! Go Jesus!" It sounded better in my head.

The guy looked at me and said, "You're on their side and you're going to burn in Hell! There's no hope for you!"

The early church didn't strive to exercise their right of free speech, because they didn't have any. It was never a battle of what they had a right to do and didn't. Rather, it was this inward motivation that they had discovered what real life was all about and they were completely committed to it. They believed in it so strongly that they formed their lives around it and did everything in their power to share this amazing new perspective of life with the people they were in community with.

THE PARABOLANI

A sustainable church model is not bigger buildings and more people. History has taught us that those things all fade away with time. What remains and stands the test of time is the Good News of Christ, and it's that Good News that we have to take to the people who have only heard and experienced bad news. People that find themselves locked in hopeless situations. We have to leave the shelter of our insulated churches that have separated us from the hurt and pain of real people living real lives, and become aware of their needs, and then meet their needs. It's only then that they will see that we really do care, and then listen to the Good News that we have to share.

In a letter to the Philippian church, Paul thanked a man that helped him by the name of Epaphroditus,[39] and in the thank you, Paul called him a *paraboleuomai*, or *parabolani*. It's translated to mean, "to risk," or, "to hazard," "to gamble." In the early church there were a group of men, part of the Christian Brotherhood, who voluntarily undertook caring for the sick and the burying of the dead. These men literally risked their lives every day by exposing themselves to contagious diseases and caring for those in prison and other high-risk situations. But they did all of it in the name of their risen Savior, Jesus Christ. They chose not to sit around in the safe and sterile environment of the spiritually passive, but rather, venture out into the world to be in and amongst those with the most needs.

The Parabolani didn't have orders or vows, but they were still numbered with the clergy of their day. They became well known for two decisive factors: their immense compassion and 'risk-taking' care of those suffering, and their zeal for which they administered hope. In AD 252 the Black Plague broke out in Carthage and the bishop commissioned a group of these "Jesus-loving-risk-takers" known as the Parabolani, and had them carry and bury the highly infectious victims of the plague, and stop the spread of it in the city. Their brave serving saved the city and stopped the spread of the disease.

Their immense compassion was powerfully balanced out by their riotous zeal. They were an active part in church controversies as the early church worked through various theological, political, and logistical issues that the fledgling movement had to face. They were one

Their immense compassion was powerfully balanced out by their riotous zeal.

of the active parties at the Second Counsel of Ephesus. They were so fanatical about what they did, and they believed that the government at that time, created laws to limit their numbers to no more than 500 in Alexandria. It was later increased, but their passion and influence to care for those outside the church body was so great, and their desire to give hope to the hopeless was so shattering to the status quo, that their actions literally altered the course of early church history.

When you look around at our modern church world, it might behoove us to have some Paraboloni's in our midst. People that love Jesus attend church and are active in making it what it needs to be. At the same time, not comfortable in just sitting and hearing the Good News, but rather living it; going out into the community and serving the neighborhoods in practical ways. It's amazing what practical help can do to turn people's view from their worries to God's greatness. Anybody can do it. There's not a lot of a requirement or hoops to jump through. You do need to be breathing, but other than that I think it's safe to say that you could make a difference in somebody's life as well.

SHERPA CHECKLIST

1. What dangers have you experienced from an inwardly focused church?

2. How important is it to take the Good News outside the church?

3. At what cost have you reached out and served others?

4. Would you classify yourself as a Jesus-lover-risk-taker?

10

GETTING OUTSIDE THE BOX

"SERIOUSLY WHAT'S THE CATCH?" SHE asked.

"No catch, it's totally free. You pull up here, and we pump $10 of gas into your car. It's free, seriously. No catch." I said with a huge smile on my face.

"Why? Why would you do that, you don't even know me."

"We are just out here trying to show people God's love in a practical way, and we all practically need gas."

I had had that exact same conversation over a hundred times that morning. The cars were lined up down the street and into the intersection causing a serious traffic jam for our little town, but nobody seemed to care when they saw the flimsy poster board sign that read, "FREE GAS." Our church had saved up several thousand dollars and decided to put it in people's gas tanks. We partnered with a gas station in a struggling area of town where the people might need a little more assistance. It was chaotic, fun, and risky all at the same time. Some people wouldn't even roll down their windows while we were pumping the gas, I guess they were scared we might be a new line of Moonies selling roses, or maybe a branch off of the Jehovah's Witness group that gave up door to door and was now witnessing car to car. There were a few people that wanted the cash instead of gas which always made me laugh, (I was born at night, but it wasn't last night.) but the majority of the people wanted to know what the catch was, and this lady was just one of those people mixed into the bunch.

When I said 'God' her entire demeanor changed. Her walls came down and so did the tears. She said, "I don't go to church and I'm not even really sure what I believe about God, if He even knows who I am or where I am, but I need a job. I have a little girl at home and bills to pay and we need to eat. I lost my job a month ago and have absolutely no money left except for twenty five cents." To which she punctuated by holding up a dirty quarter. "I finally got an interview for today in Memphis but don't have enough gas to get there. I woke up this morning and said to a God that I'm not sure exists, 'Alright God, you gotta figure something out with this gas thing because a quarter is not enough.' And I turn the corner and I see ya'll holding up a sign for Free Gas! This is freaking crazy!"

She was snot faced, and by the time she was done telling her story, I was snot faced. We filled her car up with gas and then prayed for her while the other cars sat in the Mississippi heat and waited. In that sliver of time, the gas station became holy ground. A God that she wasn't sure existed showed up in a team of ten volunteers who chose to take a weekday off and serve. She found God through the compassionate hands of a new breed of Parabolani's.

In the John 14, Jesus gave His disciples the greatest example of serving during his final meal with them; He washed their feet. During those times sandals were the most popular footwear. Prada had not yet made it to the shelves, so sandals were pretty much your only choice. Along with this limited selection of open toe footwear, came roads with plenty of dirt, dust, and animal manure. Yep, feet were nasty back in the day, and so it was customary for your feet to be washed by the lowest servant on the totem pole when you came into a house. It was not the most glamorous job to say the least, but it was a practical thing that was done before you ate, especially since during these times, meals were eaten at low reclining tables where your feet were a part of the feast whether you liked it or not. Foot-phobias were just not allowed.

During that infamous last meal, Jesus got up and washed the Disciple's feet. It was customary to have them washed before the meal, but since none of the disciples seemed to take the initiative to serve the others in this way Jesus took it upon Himself. James and John were still wondering who would get to sit on the left or the right, Peter was processing the idea of being the rock of the church, Judas was pre-occupied with how he was going to spend his new bank roll, and I doubt Thomas was paying attention.

Jesus took on the position and posture of the servant. He saw a practical need to be fulfilled and then lowered Himself to that level to serve the disciples that he had taught for years. He wrapped the towel around his waist, and then washed all of their feet, even Judas, the betrayer. When He finished, He sat back down and said "alright ya'll, I gave you an example, now you go and do the same thing."[40] Jesus Himself gave us the example of identifying a practical need, and then stepping into that need, no matter your level of social status.

> He saw a practical need to be fulfilled and then lowered Himself to that level to serve the disciples that he had taught for years.

The church I grew up in did foot washing.....like, *literal* foot washing. The women and men had to separate because we all know that every man lusts heartily after Sister Bertha's bunion infested feet. You would disrobe your sweaty feet and have them washed. Honestly, I never saw the connection or the practicality. My mom made doubly sure I was clean every time we went to church, so if I just washed my feet then why would I need somebody else to wash them again? As a young boy I never got the distant connection or practicality of this ancient practice. It just never clicked in my head why Jesus was so concerned about how clean our feet were; there had to be more to it than that. The example that Jesus was giving His disciples and us was not to have clean feet but rather to humble ourselves and serve.

The church serving was meant to be a core principle, but now it seems to be an out of the box way of thinking. Churches have become very inwardly focused with numerous saint-building programs. Isn't it interesting that the greatest teacher in the history of the world had disciples, and His idea of the best training for them was to serve others? I'm not really sure how, when or where this concept of serving slipped from the general churches repertoire, but I'm pretty sure it's due time that we get outside the box and once again begin meeting the practical needs in our communities. Some people however, have already told me that this kind of random serving in the community is a terrible idea.

> The church serving was meant to be a core principle, but now it seems to be an out of the box way of thinking.

GOATS OR SHEEP

We did a full week of various serve events in the community. There were literally numerous events every single day almost around the clock; it was exhausting, crazy, and amazing. We made sure that our church name was not on a single thing and that we didn't publicize it or try to get marketing traction from it. That was simply not our purpose or goal. Our goal was to humbly serve our community, helping those that we live alongside of, and help our own churchgoers to experience the spiritual rush of serving others. It was a wonderful week that we have duplicated numerous times since then. But after that first week of venturing out in this fashion I received an email from a concerned churchgoer from a neighboring church in our town. The email let me know that they had seen us out in town doing things to help those that were not fellow Christians. They were aghast when they discovered that we even sent a team of ladies to the local strip club to take the dancers flowers and candy. He went on to list a few more complaints and things that made his staunch biblical heritage shudder to even consider, and then he said something that I have never forgotten. He said, "If you keep doing things like this, then you will end up with a church full of goats instead of sheep, and then what condition will the church be in?" He then closed his email by saying, "I hope that you will heed my warning and realize the error of your ways."

I just love uplifting emails like that, don't you? This disgruntled person was referring to the Olivet discourse that Jesus gave in Matthew 25 where he says that on Judgment Day the Father will separate all the people as a shepherd separates sheep and goats. Of course, he totally missed the part of it that says our Heavenly Father will be doing the separating, not us. We don't have the right or the insight to know sheep from goats. Instead, Jesus sends us in a totally different direction. When Jesus was praying for His Disciples, He prayed, *"As you sent me into the world, I have sent them into the world."*[41]

Jesus was sent into the world to serve humanity at every level.[42] That's why God sent Jesus, so if Jesus was sent to serve, then guess what? We were sent to serve, not sit. Just as the Sherpa's main job is to escort people to the pinnacle of the earth, our job is to serve and escort people to the pinnacle of their lives.

This simple yet profound idea is almost the exact opposite of what is considered to be "the norm" in western churches. The majority of churches focus on feeding the flock, making proper disciples of them. But when we branch out and attempt to create a disciple, we tend to think that comes through voracious study, learning, and lots of church services. Jesus, on the other hand, made disciples by telling them to go serve. I know that studying is important, and that being an active part of a fellowship of believers is important, but if that is all we ever do, we are not actually being, or creating disciples. If we are going to be a Jesus follower then we will always end up in the world, among the goats.

SHERPA CHECKLIST

1. How often do you take the initiative to serve others when everyone else is waiting to be served?

2. Do you agree with the idea that serving is a core element of discipleship?

3. If Jesus sent us into the world to serve instead of judge, how does that change your definition of a Christian walk?

11

IT'S NOT ALL ABOUT YOU

MY WIFE, PATTI AND I have four kids. We adopted the first two and then made the second two the old-fashioned way. If you are unfamiliar with what the old-fashioned way is, please go ask your Mom. Our oldest child, we took in when she was 17, so she was pretty much already grown. However, our second child, Sierra came into our lives when she was 3 months old, so we got to experience all the joys that come with raising a small child, including temper tantrums. Have you ever seen a kid throw a temper tantrum in a store? It's crazy! You aren't sure if they need medical help or an exorcism!

The first time Sierra threw a temper tantrum I had no idea what to do. We were in a toy store buying a gift for a birthday party for another kid. I had told Sierra that she was not getting anything and that we were just going to run in and pick up a gift for her friend, and then be on our way. As I walked her through the store she picked up a stuffed unicorn and quickly decided, in her two-year-old mind, that her life could not continue without this fluffy toy. She held that silly thing all the way through the store with me repeatedly informing her that she was not going to get it.

It came time to pay for the gift and I told Sierra to put it back, and then it happened. The demon that I did not know was my child, surfaced. She fell to the floor and started kicking and screaming. I tried to pick her up but she jerked away from me, so I did what all new dads do, I walked away. The store that we were in was attached to a shopping mall, so I walked out into the main hallway where Patti was waiting on us. She saw the shocked look on my face and no child in tow.

"Where's Sierra?" She asked.

"I have no idea where she went." Which was true since the human body that I left inside the store no longer had any resemblance to the child I took into the store, but before I could offer more information, out walked Sierra in full scream. Her voice echoed off the hard polished walls of the mall and instantly filled the entire space with her blood-curdling scream. As a new dad I was completely out of my element, I did all I knew to do and that was to scoop her up like a sack of potatoes and rush her out to the car.[43]

I'm sure you have either experienced that at one time or another or at the very least seen it happen in stores across the country, and in every one of those situations, the tantrum is being thrown by the person who thinks that everything is about them. They have no concept about anything else that is going on in life except for themselves and their issues or angst.

Temper tantrums are no longer reserved just for kids. Everything has to go our way or out comes the tantrum, and if 'tantrum' is too strong of a word for you then we at least become very self-focused. Our problems and issues become all we see and all we focus on. Growing up in Michigan, our driver's training was a little bit different than other parts of the nation, and one of the lessons a young driver had to learn was that when you are driving in a snow storm, never focus on the snow, always focus on the road. If you allow your eyes to focus on the snow, which is the current issue at hand, you'll get snow blindness and drive off the road. It's almost as if you get hypnotized by the very thing you are trying to endure, so you have to focus your eyes and attention on the road in front of you not the snow that's falling.

Maybe you're reading this and you're going through a difficult time in your life, maybe even a storm or two, and you're also in the midst of your very own tantrum. Possibly a well-deserved tantrum, and the last thing you want to do is think about serving anybody else, because after all, it's in times like these that it really is all about you. When we're in the middle of a storm, society and culture tell us that we should stop everything and focus all of our attention and efforts on ourselves, and when we look at the Bible and go to the book of human storms we can possibly see the same thing.

J O B

The book of Job is by far one of the greatest stories of human misfortune ever written. But a lot of times when we read it or hear about it, all we fixate on is the epic tragedy instead of looking at the blessing at the end, and why the blessing came when it did. At the end of Job's book it says that the latter part of his life was more blessed than the former.[44] That's a fancy way of saying the dude got more blessings. In fact, double what he had before.

So what broke the onslaught of the enemy? Did the Devil give up? Did he throw in the towel?

Job endures over 30 chapters of pain, suffering, and verbal thrashing from his friends. He has lost all of his 10 kids in one day, all of his animals, and all of his money. To add insult to injury, all he is left with is a nagging wife who is quick to give up on God and sit in her own little wambulance.[45] Job endures all of this and more. He also has to put up with horrible advice from a group of friends. All of which culminates into the perfect nightmare. Job was no different than any of us. In the middle of his storm he did the same thing that we all do, and that is, ask the big 'why' questions. Why is this happening to me? Why doesn't God help? Why, why, why? Then from the middle of Job's storm God finally speaks.

It's funny, because Job desires God to speak for all these chapters, but when God finally does speak, it's not the most pleasant and encouraging of words. God says, *"Who is this that obscures my plans with words without knowledge?"* In other words, 'who is asking all of these *why* questions and doesn't know squat?' And then God says possibly my favorite scripture of all time; He says, *"Brace yourself like a man;"*[46] 'Okay boy, you think you know it all and you can handle all this stuff, let's step outside and go a few rounds!' God continues: *"I will question you, and you shall answer me. Where were you when I laid the earth's foundation? Tell me, if you understand."* Then God goes on and on posing all of these crazy, totally unanswerable questions to Job that there is literally no way he could know the answers to.

God asks him where he was when He flung the planets and stars into their places. He asks him if he can count the clouds or if he knows where He stores all the snow. He covers these large topics and then brings it down to things that are even part of Job's world and asks him if he knows where the mountain goats give birth; such an odd series of questions, from massive topics of constellations to animal birthing. But God's point is painfully clear, there is a massively huge world out there with millions of things going on all the time that you know nothing about, and all you are focused on is your small life and its small problems.

God was showing Job a glimpse of life outside himself. When Job was in the midst of his storm and throwing his tantrum, a well-deserved tantrum, but a tantrum nonetheless, he was only seeing his little world. He was only seeing his pain, and his issues, and his problems. And when we are in the middle of difficult situations or painful moments, we think it really is all about us. Everybody should be thinking about us and everybody should be commenting on our Facebook status that says, 'I'm having a bad day.' It doesn't matter what is going on in your

THE 5 ½ MILE HIGH CLUB | 107

world, it's my world that we are talking about here, and in case you didn't know, that's why I posted it on Facebook. It's not all about us, no matter what we are going through; there are things outside of our little world.

Everybody should be thinking about us and everybody should be commenting on our Facebook status that says, 'I'm having a bad day.'

After God finished His line of questioning to get Job back on the right thinking track, He then turned His attention and words to the friends that had been berating Job. God told the friends that He wasn't happy with them at all, and that they needed to go to Job, make a sacrifice for their sins and then Job would pray for them.[47]

Now that might not seem like a huge deal to you, but you need to remember or realize that these are the same friends that told Job he was living in sin and hiding it and that's why God did all these things to him. They also told Job that his kids were dead because of the sins that they had committed, and of course by that statement they were also saying that his kids were not only dead, but in Hell as well. So, put yourself in Job's shoes for just a minute. If you had a 'friend' that told you that you were a heathen and God was punishing you, even though you knew you weren't, and then told you that your kids were dead and in hell, being punished for their own grievous sins, you might be a little bit miffed at these so called friends.

If you ever want to make somebody mad, correct his or her kids. Every time someone on one of our ministry teams at church has to correct a child or a parent for keeping a crying baby in the auditorium, it's almost always difficult. Our kids have a special place in our hearts and we will always go to bat for them. Our kids are always the fastest, smartest, and best behaved. When these 'friends' insulted and demoralized Job's kids, Job got upset. The Bible doesn't say it, but I'm sure he did. He was a normal dude with normal feelings and emotions, and very much a loving and normal dad. So when God told these 'friends' to go to Job for prayer, I'm sure they were a bit concerned about what kind of prayer they were going to get.

I know what I would've prayed for them, and it wouldn't have been nice or pleasant. It would have been something along the lines of, "Lord, may the fleas of ten thousand camels inhabit the hairs of their armpits, and may their arms be too short for them to scratch!" or something like that. Praying for someone you are upset with or mad at is a difficult and humbling experience. Job probably wanted to curse them, but instead, God wanted Job to serve them. God had brought Job to the right place, at the right time, to serve the men that had cursed him.

Sherpa's are not on the mountain to judge the climbers; they're there to serve them. To do whatever is necessary to make sure they make it to the top of the world's highest peak. They don't judge, they serve. God had placed Job in a position not to judge but rather to serve.

> Sherpa's are not on the mountain to judge the climbers; they're there to serve them.

My servant Job will pray for you, and I will accept his prayer and not deal with you according to your folly. You have not spoken the truth about me, as my servant Job has." So Eliphaz the Temanite, Bildad the Shuhite and Zophar the Naamathite did what the Lord told them; and the Lord accepted Job's prayer. After Job had prayed for his friends, the Lord restored his fortunes and gave him twice as much as he had before.48

It was after Job prayed for them, that the release came. I don't know if he had messed up feelings towards them or not. I don't know what was going on in his head, but the Bible says that Job prayed for them. He served them. He provided for them the one thing that they needed at that moment. He served them, and because of that selfless act of humility, God restored Job's wealth and blessed him more

> It was Job's serving others that broke the cycle of the enemy's attack in his life.

in the upcoming days than he did before. But it was Job's serving others that broke the cycle of the enemy's attack in his life.

Serving is a powerful thing that not only helps others move forward in life, but it also breaks the enemy's attacks and the ongoing, problematic cycles in our lives. Serving is not just helping others, but in the process it helps us. It opens us up to life outside of ourselves and we realize that there is more going on in this world than just our little problems in our little world. I'm sure some of you are reading this and you're thinking to yourselves that I have no idea how massive your issues and storms in life are, and to that I would say, you're absolutely correct, I don't have a clue. However, there is no way they are worse then what Job endured, and he learned that the best way to end the cyclone in your life is to hear the voice of God and serve those around you, even if you don't like them.

Job could have just sat there taking a ride in the wambulance with his wife. He could have said, "Okay God, I can pray for these schmucks, but first I need a little relief. I need things in my life to get better before I can reach out and help them. As soon as my sickness is gone, or as soon as my finances get better, or as soon as my marriage gets stronger, then I can help somebody else." We're excellent at the 'when' game. When things get better, stronger, faster, cleaner, or richer then I will help. And so what we end up doing is nothing, because we have it backwards. We're waiting for God to act, and then once He acts, then we'll serve. But God says no, first you serve and then I will act. It's our acts of service that cause God's hand to move in our lives, not only in blessings, but also in breaking the attack of the enemy.

Everybody aspires to be great. I've never met anybody that has a goal and dream to be a poor drug addict living on the street, or in their momma's basement, but that's still where some people end up. I've also never met anybody that wants to be in a storm or a difficult place in life, yet so many people find themselves there, and then stay there. It's one thing to be in a storm, but it's a choice whether we stay in it or not. Too often we find ourselves in a difficult situation or a storm of life, and we earnestly and honestly pray and beg God to remove us from the situation or move the storm from our life. We keep doing the same things we've always done and just sit in the same storm of life year after year wondering why God is not sending legions of angels to rescue us.

Of course, we should be praying and asking God those things, that's perfectly normal, but what if there is more that we could do to see our redemption come? What if we got up in the middle of the storm and followed the example that Jesus gave us and serve somebody? If we want failure to leave and greatness to come, then one of the things that we could be actively doing in our lives to help dispel the storm is to *serve*.

Jesus told us in Matthew, *"The greatest among you will be your servant."*[49] That's a promise and a declaration for anyone and everyone. It's one thing to want to be great and to have a desire and a dream to be great, but it's another thing altogether to step into that greatness, and in order to step into that greatness we have to be willing to step out of our own self-blindness. We have to see past our own issues and not wait for them to be removed, but step in spite of them.

We've already talked about Jesus washing the disciple's feet and how that extreme example of serving was left as a model for each of us to follow in our lives. After He knelt down and washed their feet, He said this, *"Now that you know these things, you will be blessed if you do them."*[50] Now that we know serving is not just an idea, but also an actual tool that stifles the enemy in our lives and helps lead others to the top of the mountain, we will be blessed if we do it.

I don't want to hurt your feelings but it's not about you, and it's not about me. What it is all about is seeing how many people, who

> I don't want to hurt your feelings but it's not about you.

have never summited the greatest spiritual mountain in their lives, make it to the top to meet Jesus, and one of the main ways that they get there, is by following us. By seeing and hearing the journey that God has taken us on, and by allowing us to help them, and love them, and serve them to the point where they no longer see the church, or the Christians, but rather they see the loving heart of a servant; The Heart of a Sherpa.

SHERPA CHECKLIST

1. What storm have you been focusing on?

2. What or who could you focus on instead of only looking at your own issues?

3. What current issue or storm are you waiting to pass before you serve others? Why are you waiting?

NOTES

Chapter 1

1. We called everybody brother or sister even if we didn't know them. Of course, using the term brother or sister was no endearing term to an 8 year old. To me, it just made me think that at any random moment we might fight.
2. John 15:9
3. 2 Timothy 1:7
4. "This is a damnable doctrine and people should flee and regard it with horror as a dangerous plague!"

Chapter 2

5. John 10:10
6. Matthew 23:11
7. John 4:6-7 shows us that the lady came to get water at noon. This is the hottest part of the day and not the time you would normally draw water. Since the well was a central town water supply, getting water would be done in the morning and evening and would be a busy time of day, which would lend

itself to being a social time as much as a necessity. The lady in question chose to get water at a very non-social time, and at the hottest part of the day emphasizing her desire to not be in contact with her peers.

8. John 4:39 (NLT)
9. John 4:42 (NLT)
10. 1 Samuel 17:54
11. 1 Samuel 17

Chapter 3

12. Buried in the Sky: The Extraordinary Story of the Sherpa Climbers on K2's Deadliest Day. By Peter Zuckerman and Amanda Padoan
13. (MSG)
14. John 14:26 (ESV)
15. One of my theology professors taught us that the word "stuff" was a great all inclusive theology word. This could very well be the only thing I remember from his class.
16. Ephesians 1:13, 14 (ESV)
17. 1 Corinthians 12:11 (MSG)
18. Galatians 5:22-24 (ESV)

Chapter 4

19. According to the Guinness Book of World Records the Central American Cockroach, inch for inch, is the fastest animal on the planet. Their average length is between 2 and 3 inches long.
20. Galatians 2:20
21. Hebrews 11:35-37 (NLT)
22. Move. What 1,000 Churches Reveal About Spiritual Growth. By Greg L. Hawkins & Cally Parkinson

Chapter 5

23. 1 Samuel 9:18-20
24. Jeremiah 1:5
25. 1 Samuel 10:20-24 (NLT)
26. Matthew 20:26
27. Luke 22:44
28. Obviously, this is my paraphrase of the actual scriptural account found in Genesis 2:17.
29. Matthew 27:30
30. Isaiah 55:8-9
31. Matthew 5:23-26
32. New Living Translation
33. Romans 16:20 (NLT)
34. John 19:34 New International Version one of the soldiers pierced Jesus' side with a spear, bringing a sudden flow of blood and water.

Chapter 6

35. John 12:24-26
36. Mark 5:35-43, Luke 7:11-16, John 11:1-44
37. John 11:5-6

Chapter 9

38. Exodus 14:21
39. Philippians 2:25-30

Chapter 10

40. John 13:1-17 "Ya'll" is not actually in the Bible but every Southerner knows that Jesus grew up in Southern Palestine.
41. John 17:18
42. Matthew 20:28

Chapter 11

43. We moved to Honduras shortly after that incident, and while we were there a sweet older Honduran lady who we called Momma Reyes, taught us a trick that cures tantrums in one to two incidents. It was awesome! When the child starts throwing a tantrum you say, "This is a tantrum." And then you pick up that child, and hold them in a cold shower, clothes and all. I'm not talking about water boarding here, just their body writhing under the shockingly cold water. Hold them there for about five to ten seconds the whole time saying, "This is what a tantrum gets." Then the next time they start into a tantrum you just say, "Is this a tantrum?" When we did this with Sierra it cured her in one shower. She started to throw one again on another day and I just asked her if it was a tantrum and she just stopped crying and corrected herself. It was wonderful.

44. Job 42:12

45. A fictional ambulance for someone who is crying or whining about a situation that, in the big scheme of things, is really not that big of a deal.

46. Job 38:1-4

47. Job 42:7-10

48. Job 42:8-10

49. Matthew 23:11

50. John 13:17

96048877R00081

Made in the USA
Lexington, KY
15 August 2018